DAVID IVES

David Ives is the author of *All in the Timing*, *Venus in Fur* (also the film by Roman Polanski), *New Jerusalem: The Interrogation of Baruch de Spinoza*, *Lives of the Saints*, *Ancient History*, *Mere Mortals*, *Polish Joke*, *The Red Address*, *The School for Lies* (adapted from Molière), *The Liar* (adapted from Corneille), *The Heir Apparent* (adapted from Regnard), *The Metromaniacs* (adapted from Piron), *The Panties, The Partner and the One-Percent* (adapted from Sternheim), and many other works. Details and elaborations at www.davidives.net

STEPHEN SONDHEIM

Stephen Sondheim wrote the music and lyrics for *Saturday Night* (1954), *A Funny Thing Happened on the Way to the Forum* (1962), *Anyone Can Whistle* (1964), *Company* (1970), *Follies* (1971), *A Little Night Music* (1973), *The Frogs* (1974), *Pacific Overtures* (1976), *Sweeney Todd* (1979), *Merrily We Roll Along* (1981), *Sunday in the Park with George* (1984), *Into the Woods* (1987), *Assassins* (1991), *Passion* (1994), *Road Show* (2008) and *Here We Are* (2023), as well as the lyrics for *West Side Story* (1957), *Gypsy* (1959), *Do I Hear a Waltz?* (1965) and additional lyrics for *Candide* (1973). *Side by Side by Sondheim* (1976), *Marry Me a Little* (1981), *You're Gonna Love Tomorrow* (1983), *Putting It Together* (1993/99), *Moving On* (2001), *Sondheim on Sondheim* (2010) and *Old Friends* (2023) are anthologies of his work as composer and lyricist.

For films, he composed the scores of *Stavisky* (1974), co-composed the score for *Reds* (1981) and wrote songs for *Dick Tracy* (1990). He wrote songs for the television production *Evening Primrose* (1966), co-authored the film *The Last of Sheila* (1973) and the play *Getting Away with Murder* (1996), and provided incidental music for the plays *The Girls of Summer* (1956), *Invitation to a March* (1961), *Twigs* (1971) and *The Enclave* (1973).

He won the Tony Award for Best Score for *Company*, *Follies*, *A Little Night Music*, *Sweeney Todd*, *Into the Woods* and *Passion*, all of which won the New York Drama Critics' Circle Award, as did *Pacific Overtures* and *Sunday in the Park with George*, the latter also receiving the Pulitzer Prize for Drama (1985).

Stephen Sondheim was born in 1930 and raised in New York City. He graduated from Williams College, winning the Hutchinson Prize for Music Composition, after which he studied theory and composition with Milton Babbitt.

He was on the Council of the Dramatists Guild, the national association of playwrights, composers and lyricists, having served as its president from 1973 to 1981. In 1983 he was elected to the American Academy of Arts and Letters and in 1990 was appointed the first Visiting Professor of Contemporary Theatre at Oxford University. He was awarded the Kennedy Center Honors in 1993, the National Medal of Arts in 1996, the MacDowell Medal in 2013 and the Presidential Medal of Freedom in 2015.

His collected lyrics with attendant essays have been published in two volumes: *Finishing the Hat* (2010) and *Look, I Made a Hat* (2011). In 2010 the Broadway theatre formerly known as Henry Miller's Theatre was renamed in his honor, and in 2019 he became the first living artist to have a theatre named in his honor on Shaftesbury Avenue when the refurbished Queen's Theatre in London's West End was renamed the Sondheim Theatre to commemorate his ninetieth birthday, by Sir Cameron Mackintosh.

Stephen Sondheim died at his home in Roxbury, Connecticut, in November 2021, at the age of ninety-one.

HERE WE ARE

Book by
David Ives

Music and Lyrics by
Stephen Sondheim

Based on Luis Buñuel's
The Discreet Charm of the Bourgeoisie
and *The Exterminating Angel*

NICK HERN BOOKS
London
www.nickhernbooks.co.uk

A Nick Hern Book

Here We Are first published in Great Britain in 2025 as a paperback original by Nick Hern Books Limited, The Glasshouse, 49a Goldhawk Road, London W12 8QP

Here We Are book copyright © 2025 David Ives
Here We Are music and lyrics copyright © 2024 Rilting Music, Inc.
Amazing Afternoons copyright © 2025 David Ives

David Ives and Stephen Sondheim have asserted their moral right to be identified as the authors of this work

Cover image: *Here We Are* (2025) Illustration by AKA NY

Designed and typeset by Nick Hern Books, London
Printed in the UK by CPI Group (UK) Ltd

A CIP catalogue record for this book is available from the British Library

ISBN 978 1 83904 473 1

All rights reserved. Except for brief passages quoted in newspaper, magazine radio or television reviews, no part of this book may be reproduced in any form or by any means, electronic or mechanical, including photocopying or recording, or by information storage and retrieval system, without permission in writing from the appropriate publisher (for reproduction of dialogue) or the music publisher (for reproductions of lyrics). This book may not be used, in whole or in part, for the development or training of artificial intelligence technologies or systems

CAUTION Professionals and amateurs are hereby warned that all materials in this book, being fully protected under the copyright laws of the United States of America, the British Empire, including the Dominion of Canada, and all other countries of the Berne and Universal Copyright Conventions, is subject to a royalty. All rights including, but not limited to, professional, amateur, motion picture, recording, recitation, lecturing, public reading, radio and television broadcast, and the rights of translation into foreign languages, are expressly reserved. Worldwide stage rights are controlled exclusively by the authors. No professional or non-professional performances may be given without obtaining in advance the written permission of the author's representatives and paying the requisite fees or royalties. Particular emphasis is placed on the question of readings and all uses of this play by educational institutions, permission for which must be secured from the author's representative. Please contact Stephen Sondheim's representative with inquiries concerning all rights: F. Richard Pappas, Esq., 2705 Wooldridge Drive, Austin, Texas 78703.

www.nickhernbooks.co.uk/environmental-policy

Nick Hern Books' authorised representative in the EU is
Easy Access System Europe – Mustamäe tee 50, 10621 Tallinn, Estonia
email gpsr.requests@easproject.com

Contents

Amazing Afternoons: Writing with Sondheim *by David Ives*	vii
Production History	xxxix
HERE WE ARE	
Act One: The Road	3
Act Two: The Room	60

AMAZING AFTERNOONS

Writing with Sondheim

David Ives

This is for Steve.

'You never write, *you never* call...*'*

> Eliot writes me that he thinks Stravinsky is looking
> for a libretto. It would be fun, I guess, to be something
> unimportant in something wonderful.
>
> Robert Lowell, in a letter

One day in mid-December 2009, Stephen Sondheim called me up out of the blue and asked if I'd like to come over to his house sometime for a drink. He said he wanted to talk to me about something.

'It's nothing important,' he put in quickly, as if to preempt any great expectations I might start to harbor about the meeting.

Sondheim and I were acquaintances at that point, and had crossed paths the way you do in the little medieval city-within-a-city that is Theatre. I had certainly never been to his East Side townhouse. From his tone I figured he wanted to ask a favor of me: to be on a Dramatists Guild committee, or maybe to mentor a young playwright or help with some award. As it happened, I had a lot on my plate when he called me. My new play, *Venus in Fur*, had begun rehearsals at Classic Stage Company a couple of weeks before, and the following month I was to start auditions for *The Liar*, another new piece, at the Shakespeare Theatre Company in D.C. But how could I not make room for a drink with Sondheim? I said I'd be happy to come over and we set a date for an afternoon a couple of days before Christmas.

There was a weird layer of *déjà vu* in all this, because Sondheim had called me up once many years before, on what was simultaneously one of the best and worst days of my life...

In the early 1990s I had decided in the course of what can only be called a raging but unacknowledged mid-life crisis to leave Martha, The Best Girlfriend In The World, and move to San Francisco. Over the preceding three or four seasons I'd had some miniature success in New York with short comedies in the Manhattan Punch Line's annual one-act festival – plays like *Sure Thing* and *Words, Words, Words* – but I was tired of contending with a loud and filthy and inconsiderate city. One of my plays, *The Red Address*, had just been produced at the

Magic Theatre in San Francisco and, having fallen for the town while out there for rehearsals, I decided to move bag and baggage and try my fortunes amidst its fog and faded pastels.

So there I was that morning, newly moved in, in my still-pretty-bare apartment in San Francisco's Marina District. Little did I know when I took the apartment that the Marina had been built on landfill. Anyone who knows the Gospel parable about the man who built his house on rock and the idiot who built his house on sand will recognize my folly. The Marina was the worst place to be during, say, an earthquake or a mid-life crisis – as I was to learn on those nights when I lay in bed listening to the creaking of the joists as the building swayed back and forth in a temblor and a fine, sour dust from the resulting friction filled my apartment. That particular morning, though, as I was unpacking my things, everything looked new and fresh and the world seemed all before me. The technician had come just that morning to connect my new phone. What we used to call a *landline*, of course.

The new phone rang. It was Stephen Sondheim.

'What's this number?' he asked. 'It's not New York.'

'San Francisco,' I said. 'I just moved here.'

'Oh,' he said.

We chatted a bit. I didn't know him at all then and kept calling him 'Mr Sondheim' until he asked me to call him 'Steve'. I wondered what he was doing on the phone with me until he told me how much he liked my short play *Sure Thing*.

He said, 'Too bad you're in San Francisco. I had an idea for a show and was wondering if you might want to work on it.'

I can't remember now what I stammered out in response.

'Listen,' he said, 'if you ever move back to New York, give me a call.'

This is simultaneously the best and worst day of your life: a theatre god wants to collaborate on a project. Unfortunately, the god is in New York while you're camped out on a heap of shaky landfill in San Francisco. Not long after, I decided to follow up on his call. I flew to New York, staying on a friend's couch, and rang up 'Steve'.

He said, 'You didn't come all the way just to talk to me, did you?'

'No,' I said. 'No no no no no. Just visiting New York. Seeing some friends.'

'Well, I have to go into the hospital for a gall bladder'
(I think it was gall bladder) 'operation so I'm going to be out
of commission for a while. Let me know if you're ever back in
town.'

I flew back to San Francisco. Somehow Stephen Sondheim
and I seemed to keep near-missing each other.

A couple of years later, having more or less come to my
senses, I moved back to New York, picked up where I'd left off
with Martha, The Best Girlfriend In The World, and ran into
Steve at my show *All in the Timing* at the 45th Street Theatre.
He was there with his then-companion Peter Jones. (As it
happens, Martha and I would be married onstage at that same
theatre several years later, with a Mac Wellman set as the altar
of our sanctuary.) While we chatted outside at intermission,
Sondheim seemed ill at ease, even skittish, nervously avoiding
eye contact. I thought, as any playwright might in that situation,
that he hated the show. In time I'd learn that he often wore that
cornered, wary look whenever he was out in public. Still, the
vibe was so noticeable that I made an entry in my notebooks
that night:

*Stephen Sondheim came to my show. The scariest eyes I've
ever seen. His sidelong glance. The way his gaze slides away.*

Thereafter we continued to run into each other at various
events where he seemed more at ease either with himself or
with me. In 1998, Steve and I shared the Inge Playwriting
Conference Awards, he for the established master, I for the
'young' playwright – it being one of the rare kindnesses of
the theatre that even in one's late forties one can still count as
young.

During that conference in Independence, Kansas, he was
scheduled to do a talk in an auditorium early on a Saturday
morning. I was backstage with him beforehand when the
festival director asked Steve how he wanted to proceed. Steve
turned to me and said, 'Why don't you and I just go out there
and have a conversation? You can ask me how I'd turn *Hamlet*
into a musical.' So we two went onstage and it turned out to
be a funny, free-and-easy, wide-ranging conversation, all of
it luckily captured on videotape. Unfortunately, I never did
ask him how he'd turn *Hamlet* into a musical. Even more
unfortunately, when my copy of the tape arrived in the mail
some weeks later, I found that the sound guy at the Inge Festival

had neglected to turn on the volume. So somewhere in my files, I have an hour-long silent-movie of Stephen Sondheim and myself gesticulating to each other on a stage, soundlessly howling at each other's jokes.

In 2006 I was in London working on a commedia version of *The Hound of the Baskervilles* with a trio of Spanish clowns (I swear to God) when a production of *Sunday in the Park with George* was playing in the West End. Somehow Sondheim or his collaborator James Lapine heard that I was in London and invited me to come see the show. They met me outside Wyndham's Theatre just before curtain and walked me in, asking me to join them for a drink at the interval. It was a terrific production, yet at the break Steve looked glum as we went up the aisle toward the patrons' lounge.

'But Steve,' one of his producers protested, 'people were absolutely *weeping* all around me!'

'Probably your investors,' Steve said. When we got to the lounge he said to the barman, 'To quote Elaine Stritch: give me a bottle of vodka and a floor plan.' Truth to tell, Steve was delighted with that production. He was apparently just having a case of The Glooms.

What Sondheim didn't know when he called me up that December afternoon was that we had met regularly in a whole other sphere: for years I'd had recurring dreams about him. The dream usually included an invitation to a crowded dinner party at his house. Here's a typical one, from 2005:

> I was at Stephen Sondheim's house. There were many other guests, Mary Rodgers among them. Everyone there seemed to be *in* on something, however, and spoke in a way that made me think them all in some sort of strange cabal. Mary in particular was acerbic, ironic, pointed. Yet I was happy to be there with Sondheim, as always – until he told a story about someone's sexual life that was so off-putting that I wondered if he'd told it to discomfit me. Then (just as in a movie), I was looking out a window when, moving to the side, I saw something out there, saw more and more of it, and realized that it was the Eiffel Tower and that I was in Paris.
>
> Gradually I was realizing that something was wrong, but I couldn't put my finger on it. Then Martha

appeared, having just arrived in Paris, and asked me why I hadn't written her. She also asked about my original purpose in coming to Paris, which was to work with some actress. As she spoke I realized that I could remember nothing of what had happened recently. My mind had curious blanks in it. Then a woman walked up to me who murmured, 'Pass me off as your wife.' I said that I couldn't, pointing to Martha and saying that *she* was my wife. I realized that this woman was an agent of some kind, investigating this sinister group at Sondheim's house.

Then she was discovered and taken away and I knew somehow that I was being held prisoner here, was being interrogated because I had some secret about Mao (!), but that every day Sondheim was injecting me with something that would make me forget everything that had happened during the day, including my interrogation sessions. Then in the dream I began trying to escape, and this included a sequence when I was floating down the Seine at night, but I was caught by Sondheim and his flunkies and brought back. I realized that there was no escape, and that freedom was made harder by these blanks in my memory, by this daily forced amnesia. So I devised a plan: on a strip of paper I wrote a note to myself that said, 'BELIEVE NOTHING OF WHAT YOU SAY', and I tucked that away in my pocket for tomorrow. I would read it and be made aware of my situation and somehow be able to free myself, to escape...

In any case, there I was – not in a dream – on the doorstep of Sondheim's townhouse on East 49th Street on the appointed December afternoon when he 'wanted to talk to me about something'. The entrance to his house was through a gate and down a couple of steps to the front door. Through an old metal speaker on the doorpost, Steve Clar, Sondheim's long-time assistant, asked who I was, then came down from his eyrie in the upper floors to let me in.

(I always thought it a wonderful touch that Stephen Sondheim, famous for the clarity of his work, had an assistant a) named 'Steve' and b) named 'Clar' – as if 'Steve Clar' were some superbly efficient, doppelgängling avatar, a shock-haired column of protoplasm who answered Steve's phones and managed his calendar for him. Also, consider that Stephen Sondheim was universally known as 'Steve'. Could Ludwig van Beethoven ever have been known as 'Lou'? Richard Wagner as 'Dick'?)

Past the building's front door, you entered a brief, low, closed foyer paneled in rich brown wood with a turquoise-blue tiled ceiling – a sort of artful miniature mosaic sky. Beyond the door at the far end you walked straight into the living room, where that day no doubt – as would always happen – one or both of Steve's full-size black poodles jumped all over me as I entered. To the right, a pale-wood staircase bent toward to the upper floors. To the left stood a well-stocked liquor cabinet. In the far corner, by the back windows, a handsome old card table looking out on Turtle Bay Gardens. On the walls and shelves of the room, Steve's collection of antique and modern puzzles and games were on display.

Sondheim poured out drinks and we chatted for a while, he on the couch and I on a chair next to a cabinet atop which sat a wonderful sculpture of a little girl unfurling a rippling, horizontal, suspended-by-nothing bronze cloth in a strong invisible wind. (A fine metaphor for Art, now that I think of it.) Sondheim at this point in his life was seventy-nine and still looked, if portly, very hale, though as he got up to pour a second round he already had the rolling, half-falling, precarious gait that would get more precarious over the years. With that second drink, enough time and chitchat had passed for me to notice that Sondheim still hadn't brought up the reason for my visit.

I said, 'So, Steve, what did you want to talk about? You said it wasn't important.'

'Did I say that?' he snapped out as if impatient with himself for having said so.

'That is what you said,' I said.

Here's where I expected him to ask me to mentor a playwright or help at a benefit.

'Actually,' he said, 'I've had this idea for a musical for years. I wondered if you'd be interested in working on it.'

Significant pause. What does one say to that?

I said, 'What's the idea?' – quietly remembering San Francisco and registering that this was the second time in my life we'd had a conversation which started like this. On this occasion, we were in the same city instead of on the phone and fifteen years had passed.

He said, 'It's a musical I call *All Together Now...*'

As he described the show that afternoon, it was to center on two characters, a man and a woman, probably married, or maybe headed for marriage, maybe with children. The action would show the disintegration of the couple's relationship over several scenes, or possibly disintegration followed by reunion, the action covering years of time.

Most crucially: surrounding the pair there would be two acting-singing-dancing choruses comprised respectively of the man's and woman's Inner Selves. ('Inner Selves' was Sondheim's own term to describe them.) The Selves, each of them representing some emotion or attitude or element or trait in that character, would let us see what was going on underneath the dialogue, would reveal who these two people were below the surface, would show their hidden emotional conflicts, disclose their well-concealed *un*-togetherness. The Selves would also demonstrate how aspects of our characters can sabotage us, countering our best interests. In Steve's imagining, the Inner Selves would enter as a mob, rushing in, shouting 'HELP! HELP! HELP!' He foresaw one male, dangerous Inner Self who carried a knife or a gun. That dangerous self he always conceived of as physically disabled in some way – limping, perhaps. He thought that that threatening Self might be murdered by the other male Selves late in the plot, representing the liberation of our central male character.

He thought the musical part of the show would probably belong to the Inner Selves rather than the two main characters, but he had not settled on that for certain. One thing he was sure of: at the very end, all of the conflicting Selves would somehow come into harmony, the man and the woman's inner conflicts and outer problems would resolve, and everyone (possibly the man and woman as well) would sing a finale titled 'All Together Now'. Maybe at the very last moment there'd be just a hint of discord, to show that all is *not* quite together. In other words, an ending that was typically ambiguous, typically Sondheim.

When he'd finished outlining his concept, I said, truthfully, 'I like this idea.'

Sondheim mentioned that he'd approached other playwrights about this show over the years. (In an interview from 2017 that

I didn't see till after he'd died, Steve said he had approached Craig Lucas and Terrence McNally. There may have been others.) I wondered if *All Together Now* had been the reason for the San Francisco call those many years before. It was certainly lucky we hadn't attempted to work on it at that point because I wouldn't have been ready back then to take on anything this complex. In fact, it was only after Steve and I started work that I realized just how daunting a concept *All Together Now* could be to realize. That afternoon, I was blithe.

I threw out some questions about his idea, we brainstormed a bit off the top of our heads, and then he said: 'I've taken some notes…'

He dug a manila envelope out of the pillows of the couch he was sitting on and handed it across to me.

'Why don't you take those home and read them over, see if you still like the idea, and if you do we can meet again and talk.' He checked his watch. 'I have to go to the theatre.'

'You've got a car waiting?'

'A *car*?' he said, and let out that sudden, deafening laugh I was to get to know so well. 'You've got the wrong guy. That's Arthur Laurents. I'm taking a cab.'

(Actually, Steve liked a car and driver as much as anybody, especially as time went on. I think he just wanted to get in that typical affectionate dig at Arthur Laurents. When I had to have a meeting with Laurents about adapting *Anyone Can Whistle* for Encores and asked Steve for advice on how to deal with his famously adder-tongued collaborator, Steve said, 'Just tell Arthur you love his work. He'll ask you to marry him.' As for that laugh, it was so unmistakable, so characteristic of Steve that actors in shows always knew instantly when he was in the audience, as That Laugh came out of the dark.)

As I packed up to leave, it turned out that the manila envelope he'd given me didn't fit comfortably into the briefcase I was carrying. I had to force it a little to get it in.

'Bad omen,' he said.

'Small briefcase,' I said.

At home I read the notes over and over and wrote a lengthy response that I emailed to Steve. We talked on the phone and set a date after the first of the year to begin.

*

> I really don't know how poetry gets to be written.
> There is a mystery and a surprise, and after that a great
> deal of hard work.
>
> Elizabeth Bishop

Just to clarify: I am not an expert on, or even much of a follower of, musicals. Before 1993, when I started adapting old and/or neglected musicals for the Encores series at City Center (ultimately I would adapt thirty-three of them), I'd probably seen half-a-dozen musicals in my whole life. Two of those shows were *Sweeney Todd* in its original production. One was *Sunday in the Park with George*. Pinter and Albee and Beckett embodied my idea, and my ideal, of theatre. So when Steve and I started work on *All Together Now*, my entire musical resumé consisted of my Encores adaptations to that date, the libretto for a children's opera that had premiered in Philadelphia twenty years previously, a small out-of-town musical I'd written with Phyllis Newman using Comden and Green songs, and *White Christmas* and *Dance of the Vampires* on Broadway. (Yes, *Dance of the Vampires*, which I believe at the time constituted the most expensive flop in Broadway history. There's a funny and instructive book to be written about working on the production. I don't want to write it.) I had also once written a five-minute-and-thirty-eight-second-long *a capella* 'musical' for four performers called *Philip Glass Buys a Loaf of Bread* that was part of *All in the Timing*, the show that Steve saw at the 45th Street Theatre.

Steve didn't seem to mind my lack of musical-theatre chops. But then, Sondheim's shows were never your standard musicals and his collaborators were never the usual suspects. George Furth, the bookwriter of *Company*, was an actor. John Weidman of *Pacific Overtures*, *Assassins* and *Road Show* has a law degree. James Lapine of *Sunday in the Park with George*, *Into the Woods* and *Passion*, started out in graphic design. Musical bookwriters are generally (in fact, they're literally) un-sung, but Steve was always quick to acknowledge the contributions of his collaborators in letters to editors. With me, whenever praising Weidman's gifts as a writer, Steve would add, 'Weidman is also the best man in the world.' (True.) Of Lapine, he would always say that Lapine was *a poet*. His example was the Soldier's line from *Sunday in the Park with George*, 'I like the one in the light hat.'

'The *LIGHT* hat,' Steve would say. 'Not the *white* hat, the *light* hat. That is a poet.'

Soon after Steve and I started meeting, I noted that our forward progress quickly got slowed or interrupted by various ailments and excuses on his part, some serious (trips to London on business), some not (trips to dinner with friends), and quickly realized that, where writing was concerned, Stephen Sondheim was a master procrastinator. Steve knew it himself. In a *New Yorker* interview taped in 2014, an interview in which Sondheim first spoke publicly about our collaboration, Adam Gopnik asked if Steve had any dream projects.

Steve answered, 'My idea of a dream project is not writing.'

He once claimed to me that he couldn't work on our show because of an ingrown toenail. In fact, he instructed me at length and in detail on how to trim my own toenails so as to avoid that particular affliction. In a sort of comic twist on Proust's *madeleine*, I have never since then trimmed my toenails without Stephen Sondheim materializing in my consciousness rather like Marcel's grandmother out of Proust's cup of *tisane*. Those toenail-clipping instructions, given to me during one of our meetings, were themselves procrastination. But any excuse not to work would work for Steve.

Early in the process I asked Lapine for advice and he told me I had to give Steve deadlines. James is fortunate in being constituted by nature to push someone like that. I am not. An old girlfriend of mine used to call me – it wasn't a compliment – *an allower*. Of course, with his electron-microscope insight into people's character, Sondheim may have instantly recognized me for what I was, the way alcoholics will spot potential love interests who'll let them drink: I was the partner who'd let Steve get away with not writing. At that point in his life and career, maybe an enabler and not a collaborator was what, in his heart of hearts, he wanted. Would it have made any difference if I had thought or known that? Of course not.

Sometimes when I'd push him about writing, he'd put on a comic whining voice and say, 'Hey. *I'm an old man!*'

Once, I countered that with, 'Verdi was eighty-five when he wrote *Falstaff*.'

Steve said, 'I hate Verdi.'

As time went on, and Steve and I continued making notes without any music appearing, I began to worry. We knew what many of the numbers were going to be, we knew the shape of them and which characters would sing them. It was just a matter of writing them. I'd tell Steve to just pick a spot, any spot and write the number for it.

'I have to have the whole thing in my head first,' he'd say. 'It's my German mind.'

We talked on the phone all the time, often late at night, and for long stretches we spoke every day. My phone would ring and I'd hear anything from 'Sondheim here!' to 'Are you decent?' If at the end of the conversation he said, 'Let's talk tomorrow at noon', he'd always pronounce it *nyoon*, with a satirical emphasis, because that was the affected way Ethel Merman used to say it in the days of the late 1950s when Steve was working with her on *Gypsy*. '*Let's talk at nyooon*' became a regular line between us. Later on, after iPhones came in, the caller ID on my phone would identify Sondheim as 'Unknown', an irony we both appreciated.

'Hello, Unknown,' I'd greet him.

At the beginning I was at his house quite regularly. I'd pass through the gate, I'd ring, Clar would ask who I was through the metal box, and the poodles would jump on me. Generally, we met in Steve's study on the second-floor back of his house, in what I would call a sun porch, he lying or sitting on the antique ship-captain's bed that – like many of the strange, terrific objects lying around the house – his close pal and *Forum* collaborator Burt Shevelove had given him decades before. The mattress on the antique captain's bed, which looked almost as antique as the bed itself, was always deep in scattered papers and books that wanted Steve's immediate attention. The mess itself was a still-life portrait of procrastination.

I soon got used to the ever-changing pile of puzzle books by the toilet in the second-floor bathroom. In time, Steve got me to take up cryptics, the insidious British crosswords that seem to be the brainchild of brilliant reclusive cranks from MI6. Steve himself had constructed a number of cryptics for *New York Magazine* many years before, and gave me a copy of his collected puzzles. Like his shows, each puzzle was unique, with its own set of instructions. Some were not in the traditional square, they were in circles or spirals or ad hoc geometric shapes.

In time, Steve asked how I was faring with his cryptics.

'Steve,' I said, 'the *instructions* for your puzzles are incomprehensible.'

The start of every meeting was inevitably a quarter of an hour of chatter and dish: theatre gossip, movies or shows we'd seen, stories from the past, people he'd known. (He'd met everybody.) It was a recurring regret of his that when he worked on the TV show *Topper* as a young man in the early '50s, he had never asked Lee Patrick, the wife in the show, about her experience playing Humphrey Bogart's immortal secretary Effie in *The Maltese Falcon*. We shared tastes in music, both of us equal fans of everyone from Astor Piazzolla to Arvo Pärt. Movies were also an instant and powerful bond between us. Thanks to my movie-loving father, I knew obscure films and second- and third-level performers out of the '30s and '40s, so Steve and I would entertain each other by rattling on about Albert Bassermann or Linda Darnell or Frank McHugh.

His views on movies and shows were always as original and unexpected as his works.

I said to him, 'I watched *The Razor's Edge* again last night. Tyrone Power and Gene Tierney are both so beautiful you don't know which to look at.'

'It's not surprising,' he said. 'They have the same overbite.'

Another time, commenting once on the characters in some current play or other, he said, 'They're despicable – like the main characters in Shakespeare tragedies.'

He disliked or, maybe more precisely, despised opera. The only opera I ever heard him praise was *Wozzeck*, Alban Berg's expressionistic portrait of a half-crazed soldier who murders his girlfriend. Though I'm not an opera maven, I once urged Steve to try *The Marriage of Figaro*.

'You're not the first,' he said. 'I put it on once to see what all the fuss was about and for about twenty minutes I kept thinking, "This is the greatest piece of musical theatre ever!" The problem is, then they *kept on singing*. And singing. And singing...'

'But it's charming. It's delightful,' I said.

'If there's any word I *hate*, it's "*charming*",' he said. 'Followed by "*delightful*".'

Of course, he used 'charming' and 'delightful' to describe shows all the time. Then he would apologize for having used them.

Despite the dish and the chatter and the jokes, meetings were often productive, some of them thrilling. I have an entry in my calendar on May 21, 2010 that says '1:00 Steve S.' Next to that is an annotation from later that day, circled in red pencil:

'AMAZING AFTERNOON.'

He took notes on legal pads or, less often, on a laptop. He often sipped white wine from what looked like a juice-glass (Montrachet was his favorite), the drink often replenished by his cook and loyal friend Mary Pat, who was usually cooking dinner downstairs while we worked. Sometimes, especially early on, he sipped vodka, also regularly replenished. How he could work while drinking anything – he was also no stranger to cannabis – remained a mystery to me. But who was I to question Stephen Sondheim's process?

I would pull up a chair and sit more or less in the portal of the shallow sun porch. Between us was a coffee table filled with *tchotchkes*, many of them mementoes from his shows: a miniature jigsaw puzzle of a detail from Seurat's *La Grande Jatte*, for example. Just to my left was a low bookcase with a massive old dictionary splayed open on top of it, the bookcase's shelves bulging with reference books. Just to my right, the resting place for my coffee was his piano bench. The royal ass of Leonard Bernstein had sat on that bench. It was one of Bernstein's old pianos.

On the piano top, framed, was a copy of the manuscript first page of the piano concerto Bernard Herrmann wrote for the mad composer in the 1945 thriller *Hangover Square,* one of Steve's favorite flicks. As a fifteen-year-old he'd gone to see it over and over, till he could bash out the chords of that concerto. Also on the piano top sat a framed picture of Margaret Sullavan, one of his favorite film actresses. Steve could do a spot-on comic imitation of her memorable voice, hoarsely and tearfully gasping out, 'Doctor… Doctor… Is it… *cancer*?' He had a number of studio photos of Sullavan, and rotated them in the frame on the piano 'weekly', he said.

Just beyond Steve, the high, curving stained-glass windows that formed the end of the room looked out on the gardens of Turtle Bay. Katherine Hepburn had once lived right next door – and had complained about the noise he was making on the piano. He jokingly admitted to being miffed that East 49th Street had been named 'Katherine Hepburn Place' by the city.

He said, 'I want a street sign that says Stephensondheimplatz. Spelled p-l-o-t-z.'

Later in our process, when he had finally started work on an opening number for our show, he'd sit down and play what he'd written since our last meeting while I turned the music pages. My calendar for February 9, 2012, says, '*Amazing day – SS played a bit of 'All Together Now' for me.*' I remember that after he'd played it, I told him – truthfully – that it was terrific.

He said, 'Thank you for your enthusiasm.'

I thought he was being ironic, then saw from his face that he wasn't. He would say 'Thank you for your enthusiasm' to me many times over the course of years as he brought in bits of score. Do we think Michelangelo said that? 'Ah, you like the Sistine Chapel? It's all right? Thank you for your enthusiasm!' Still, he was never shy about appreciating his own shows. He once told me that Marianne Elliott's production of *Company* was 'the greatest evening of musical theatre I've ever seen'.

Hepburn may have had good reason to complain about the noise, because the walls really were pretty thin for a tony townhouse in Turtle Bay. Once, when we were in the midst of some work, Steve sprang up from the captain's bed, ran to the piano and started banging out random dissonant chords, crashing his forearms down on the keys *molto fortissimo*. He was like Laird Cregar as the deranged composer in the mad scene from *Hangover Square.* Steve stopped to listen, thundered out a few more chords, listened, thundered out some more, then stopped and quietly returned to his place on the captain's bed.

'What was *that* about?' I said.

He said, 'The house next door is for sale. I heard some prospective tenants moving around in there. I want to dissuade anyone from buying it.'

In certain practical respects, Sondheim and I were opposites. He worked late at night and often well into the night; I work in the morning and early afternoon. But there were more serious stylistic differences. I hate stage directions, for example, and limit them to entrances, exits and crucial actions like '*She takes out a gun and shoots him.*' Similarly, I don't like telling actors how to say a line, avoiding parentheticals such as '*with a wry smile*' or '*aggressively*' or (worst) '*looking at him*'. I like actors to surprise me, always figuring that if the emotion and the action are not implicit in the dialogue then I haven't done my job.

Steve preferred to dictate and notate every nuance. He liked to quote Mies van der Rohe's line that 'God is in the details', and embodied the principle in his finical, clinical, sometimes exasperating attention to minutiae.

But who was I to take issue with Stephen Sondheim's process?

I would take handwritten notes of every work session or every phone call, type them up and send them to Steve for comment. I sent him drafts of scenes and he would not only mark them up, he'd rewrite or add some dialogue, or some jokes, of his own.

By nature, Steve was a great enthusiast. His favorite word for things he liked was 'swell'. It was one of several beautiful slang holdouts from earlier decades in his conversation, like the way he'd sometimes say, 'I dig, I dig.' Steve was also, to use Saul Bellow's term, a world-class noticer. He grilled me over the years about where I came from and what I ate and drank and about my parents and my wife and about the way I spoke, about why I didn't sound (to him) as if I'd come from Chicago, about the difference between the way he pronounced 'orange' (*aah*runge) and the way I pronounced it (*orr*inge). He once got very interested in a sweater I was wearing and interrogated me about it. It was the kind of character detail he'd write into a show.

He seemed not to care much what he himself wore. I never saw him formally dressed even on formal occasions. In our sessions he was usually in a none-too-fresh T-shirt, often snowflaked with dandruff, and a pair of loose pants and a set of Merrell's without socks. Often a wide stretch of bare pale stomach would come into view as he slouched back more and more on the captain's bed and the T-shirt rode up. Yet his hair and beard always tended to be well-kempt. Sometimes I'd breeze into our meetings saying, 'Hiya, handsome.' It never failed to tickle him.

His interest in my sweater that day was actually key to the way Steve wrote. If there was one thing I learned about his 'process', it's that – despite the wit and intelligence in his work that made some critics peg him as cerebral – he could only write a number on the basis of the character, and from that character's *details*. He would bombard me with questions about our two protagonists: specifics about where they had come from, what their lives and jobs and the places they lived in were like, what the exact circumstances were while they were singing the song.

Once, he told me to dash off a couple of monologues to clarify our main characters' voice and background.

'Don't try to make it perfect,' he said. 'Just rattle anything off. Top of your head. It's just fodder.'

I did as told, generating pages of monologue as rough 'fodder', only to have him interrogate me in depth about the material – and take issue with some punctuation. I never thereafter 'rattled off' *anything*. We did, though, continue to differ on punctuation. Our ellipses remained in constant battle to the end, as did our tortuous semi-colons.

Oddly, given the sublimity of his lyrics, Sondheim was not a reader. By his account, he had read *Ulysses* at Williams College, but not many novels since, though he did once give me a list of his six favorite mysteries, which I duly consumed to investigate his taste in detective stories. He asserted many times that he didn't understand poetry, although he remembered loving Eliot and Stevens in college. To test his poetry tone-deafness, I once gave him a simple and straightforward Philip Larkin poem called 'The Trees'. He claimed to find it mystifying.

Sometimes acutely and hilariously critical, he could also be a great *relisher*. There was the way, after decades of working toward it, after being underappreciated or misunderstood or derided, he relished his own celebrity. When he turned eighty, and there were seemingly weeks of celebrations around town, I gave him a bottle of wine. He checked the label and nodded.

'This is good stuff,' he said.

'Well,' I said, 'you don't turn eighty every day.'

'Apparently,' he crowed, 'you *can*!'

He could even send himself up. When I once took issue with some dialogue he'd written, he said, putting on a whining voice, 'Hey! Come on! *I'm an icon of the American musical theatre!*' He enjoyed his hard-won celebrity the same way he enjoyed the fact that the only rhyme for 'Sondheim' was 'Trondheim', a city on a Norwegian fjord.

He displayed the good manners of someone brought up in the American middle class before our current age of incivility and was, to a fault, thoughtful and generous. To this day I adhere to one of Steve's ethical principles: if you can afford a ticket, you don't accept a comp. Interestingly, during these same years I also worked with Roman Polanski on the film of *Venus in Fur*, and I would use similar adjectives to describe Roman: generous, funny, very smart, very detailed, beautiful manners.

Sondheim laughed louder and faster than anyone I'd ever met, and cried faster, too. Sometimes in conversation while he was talking about a movie or a song (not necessarily his own) or an event in his life, his voice would tremble and his eyes fill with tears.

'*Awwww*,' he'd say, 'I'm gonna cry.'

Steve had a reputation for being 'difficult'. I myself never saw that side. He certainly did demand precision from performers. I watched him coach singers to make sure all the flats were flat and the sharps were sharp at the Encores production of *Anyone Can Whistle*. Yet he could also appreciate what unexpected magic a performer could bring to a song. When the cast album of the movie of *Into the Woods* was being recorded, he told me that every time Meryl Streep went through the Witch's song, she did it slightly differently.

'But every time,' he said, 'it was *right*.'

He was a born teacher and loved doing for young artists what Oscar Hammerstein had done for him: instructing them in their craft. Yet he could overstep. Once, when I'd adapted an old French verse comedy, he asked for a copy of the script, only to send it back to me with the rhymes he didn't approve of marked in red. Another playwright might have been honored/grateful. I'm sorry to say I am not that playwright. There's also a line between helpful comment and covert sabotage. I was pissed off with him about his red markings for days. It was the most difficult moment of our whole time working together – in fact, the only difficult moment that comes to mind. He realized his overstep and apologized and we moved on.

He certainly could make summary judgments and hold nuclear opinions.

'Have you seen the Amy Winehouse documentary?' I asked him. 'It's terrific.'

'Yeah, Lapine said I should watch it, too.'

'It's like contemporary Greek tragedy, watching this lost woman get more and more lost heading for disaster.'

A week or so later I asked him if he'd watched it.

'I managed fifteen or twenty minutes,' he said.

'You didn't like it?'

He said, 'She didn't seem worth saving.'

*

> A line will take us hours maybe;
> Yet if it does not seem a moment's thought,
> Our stitching and unstitching has been naught.
>
> William Butler Yeats, 'Adam's Curse'

Charlie Chaplin said that whatever movie he made had to feel as natural as water rippling over pebbles in a stream. In the theatre, while great dialogue and wit and passion can make for crackle, what makes words and songs and scenes '*ripple*' is structure – each sentence and scene and song constructed correctly and arriving in the right order. A good musical book is like a well-designed house in which the rooms lead comfortably and logically one into the other; the score is the party that happens in the house. The bookwriter provides the occasion; the score provides the event. That's the job of the bookwriter – to create structure, the 'stitching and unstitching' Yeats talks about, that has to seem 'a moment's thought'. As I knew from adapting shows for Encores, musicals have often failed not because of a weak score but because a show's structure is clumsy. If the rhythm, the larger underlying rhythm of the show is off, even terrific numbers won't 'land'.

The structural design of a show, the need for *ripple*, reaches down into every element. Structuring the book and the score is the start; rehearsal then structures the rhythmic flow of thoughts and emotions radiating from the actors. Though every performance will be different in certain particulars, the actors have to hold onto the deeper structure, the rhythm that they perfected in rehearsal, or the show will go 'off'. It won't ripple. Because rhythm works invisibly and most people (including most theatre 'critics') don't know what bookwriters do or how important they are, librettists often go unmentioned or unappreciated. Not so with Steve, who religiously acknowledged the contributions of his collaborators. If the bookwriter's name was omitted from a discussion or an article or review, he would un-omit it.

We went through many versions of how to structure *All Together Now*. In the beginning, he thought the show was about a marriage, imagining that we would see the Inner Selves of two married people and follow their disintegration as a couple.

Ultimately, we decided that watching two unmarried people get together, rather than two married people fall apart, would be more compelling. Also, instead of spreading the action out over years, we decided to concentrate it into a single meeting.

There were also specifics to be addressed. Who are this man and this woman at the center of the show? Do they have names and histories or are they anonymous, a featureless Everyman and Everywoman? Who or what are the Inner Selves? How do they work? Are they specific characters, with histories of their own, or generalized 'humors'? What are the songs, the numbers, the dances? *Are* there dances? Is there a plot? What is this show *about*? Other questions revolved around dramaturgical mechanics: how to hold the audience's interest, how to keep this from being a standard guy-meets-girl relationship story, how to make the thing surprising. And most crucially: how do you keep the show from being a bunch of side characters who simply speak (or sing) the main characters' subtext aloud?

After all our discussions about where to place the action, in the end Steve and I decided on an airport bar in the middle of the night. Set elements might be added to the bar but we would always remain inside it. A bed, for example, might slide onstage for a fantasy sex scene but it would still be the bar. The back of the airport bar might suddenly become a wall of mirrors, multiplying our two main characters and their manifold Inner Selves at some moment when they were least 'together' – and implying that there were millions of Selves to deal with. In terms of the show's idea, the set functioned like a human body. One never escaped it, and it contained everything including our deepmost selves, our fantasies, our inner beds.

Part One of the show would be a brief, two-character, one-act play in several quick scenes performed 'dry', that is, without any music. After every brief scene, we jump some minutes to show the next stage in the relationship between our two main characters. In scene one, they meet as strangers in the middle of the night in our airport bar and exchange a bit of small-talk. We jump to the next scene, with him buying her a drink. We jump to a scene in which they're really getting on nicely and having fun. We jump to her pouring her heart out. We jump to the man propositioning the woman. Then, suddenly, everything freezes. *Music begins* for the first time. The Inner Selves enter and Part Two begins as we 'rewind' to the top of the show.

The same one-act we just watched before begins all over again. The dialogue is exactly as it was, but now their talk is intermixed with music – songs and dances performed by the actors portraying the man and woman's Inner Selves. Steve called these numbers 'explosions', because they shattered and investigated a single moment between our two characters. Part Two would thus musicalize and enlarge upon the music-free first act. At the end it would pick up the plot where it had broken off at the moment when the man propositions the woman, and would complete the action by showing us what happens to our couple. In other words, the show was to be a one-act followed by a musicalization or 'explosion' of that one-act.

The mere fact that Steve came up with this particular conceit for a show, with its vision of warring, compartmentalized psychic elements, some of them unappealing or unattractive or disturbing or needing to be killed off – as well as the fact that he'd contemplated this idea for years – seems to intimate that he wanted to explore his own inner life, or inner selves. From the very first notes he handed me that December afternoon I was astonished at how deeply he'd thought about the mechanics and psychology of character. In fact, there were four long, quite dense quotations in those original notes from unidentified analysts about the structure of the psyche.

Steve and I had been at work for a few years on *All Together Now* when he called me and said there was a show in previews called *First Date* that sounded a lot like our show. He suggested I go see it.

I went to the show and it was indeed (vaguely) like a version of his idea. I didn't think it was an impediment but Steve thought they'd foxed us. So we shelved *All Together Now*, although we returned to it a few years later before shelving it yet again for good. The bits of score and the pile of our notes went into a manila envelope of their own, much larger than the original manila envelope Steve had handed me. The whole project went into a corner of my writing room, where it remains. In truth, another entertainment eventually showed up that really was Steve's idea: the 2015 Pixar animated movie *Inside Out*, in which a girl's emotions – many of them unattractive – are personified and she has to deal with them.

Whether Steve would have *ever* finished *All Together Now* is a question. There's that possibly apocryphal tale of Emperor

Joseph II saying to Mozart at an opera premiere, 'Too many notes, Herr Mozart, too many notes!' *Too many notes* may have been our problem in a different sense. The pages and pages of questions and investigation for *All Together Now* certainly helped us figure the show out in the early stages. After a while, though, producing notes seemed to become an end in itself, a way for Steve to spin out the process and avoid writing. In the end I was begging Steve just to write something, write anything, a few words that he could fix or change. He always said he just didn't work that way.

'It's my German mind,' was the inevitable reason.

In retrospect, *All Together Now* – a shotgun marriage of *Brief Encounter*, *Strange Interlude* and a Renaissance comedy of humors – was probably unworkable. But then, so is the concept for a musical about presidential assassins, or a barber who kills his clients and turns them into meat pies, or about a pointillist painting. Given the way Steve held onto the idea over the course of years, there must have been something intensely personal in that story of characters besieged by, and trying to come to terms with, conflicting and sometimes destructive Selves. It's but a small alphabetical step from 'Steve' to 'Selves'.

Steve and I weren't idle after we laid *All Together Now* aside in 2013. He wanted us to continue writing and, as it happened, he had already pitched to me another idea for a show.

*

> For the first time in my life I'd come into contact with a coherent moral system that, as far as I could tell, had no flaws. It was an aggressive morality based on the completely rejection of all existing values. We had other criteria: we exalted passion, mystification, black humor, the insult, and the call of the abyss.
>
> Luis Buñuel on surrealism, in *My Last Sigh*

Steve's new idea was to base a musical on two movies by the great Spanish film director Luis Buñuel. *The Discreet Charm of the Bourgeoisie* would provide the material for Act One and *The Exterminating Angel* for Act Two. I leapt at the idea, partly because we now had something to use as a basis on which to hang the story and the characters instead of having to make everything up, as we'd had to do with *All Together Now*. Also, Buñuel was already a long-time idol of mine. Starting in the late 1920s with the groundbreaking short film *Un Chien Andalou* (made in collaboration with his friend Salvador Dalí), he had created films unlike anyone else's: deadpan, irrational, satirical, anticlerical, always with a subtle air of erotic fetishism, and always subversive. In other words, surreal.

I say that this Buñuel project was 'Steve's idea', but not long after we started work on it, I ran into James Lapine, who said to me, wryly – and pointedly – 'I hear you're working on *my musical*.' James claimed that the concept for the show had actually been his, many years before. The problem was, Steve and I were already writing. With guilty apologies to James, I continued. Later, I would read that Hal Prince claimed *he* had come up with the idea. There may be many other such claimants rattling around the Great White Way.

The Discreet Charm of the Bourgeoisie, which won the foreign film Oscar in 1973, was shot in color in France and has the bright, empty look of the commercial comedies from the period. The plot, such as it is, concerns a circle of well-heeled friends who repeatedly go in search of a meal but basically never succeed in eating. Once, they go to a fancy restaurant only to discover a funeral in progress in the back room. Once, the waiter at a café informs them there is no food. Once, two of the characters decide on the spur of the moment to have sex, stymieing the rest of the group's meal plans. Along the way, a priest shows up out of nowhere, looking for a job as a gardener. The three central male characters turn out to be running drugs. A young woman revolutionary tries to kill one of the group. All of this transpires in Buñuel's matter-of-fact, never-apologize-never-explain style.

The Exterminating Angel, from 1962, is a radically different film, although the main characters are once again a set of moneyed friends. Shot in silky black-and-white in Mexico, the action begins with a late-night dinner party in a posh mansion, with fifteen or twenty friends in evening gowns and tuxes, all spouting society chatter. After dinner, they retire to the mansion's luxurious salon…

…and there they stay. They more or less decide, amid growing anxiety, that they *can't* leave the room. Although nothing is stopping them from crossing the threshold and going home, they decide they're 'trapped'. The film follows them in that salon over days and days while the room, the situation – and they – deteriorate. Starving and unkempt, they finally manage to escape the room, only to find themselves in a Sunday-morning congregation 'trapped' inside a church. In the final moments we hear gunfire in the distance. Has a revolution broken out? Buñuel doesn't say. The last we see is a flock of sheep heading for the church.

A restaurant hosting a funeral. An open, unlocked room one somehow can't get out of. Either of these could be moments from a dream, but Buñuel doesn't present them or treat them as dreams. He films everything as 'reality', the same way Magritte paints a locomotive steaming out of a fireplace as reality. The irony of my working on this project was that I had had those recurring dreams about Sondheim for years. Now I was adapting Buñuel's cinematic dreams in company with Sondheim. It was a 'dream project' – literally.

Around this time, Steve invited my wife and me to take part in an 'Escape the Room' party he organized. We all met at an office building in the West 30s, got locked into a pseudo-Victorian parlor, and had to find clues to get out within the allotted hour. It was fitting. What is *The Exterminating Angel* but a version of 'Escape the Room'?

Structurally, merging *Discreet Charm* and *Exterminating Angel* and making the two circles of friends into the same circle made sense. In Act One they'd look for food; in the second act they'd find a meal but would be 'trapped' in a room with each other. The two stories were united around a common theme of frustrated desire, whether the desire is to eat or to leave a room. Steve and I liked the social satire, we liked the juxtaposition (so common in Sondheim shows) of a quick, bright first act with a darker second act, and we liked the topicality of food and restaurants given all the 'foodies' and food-adjacent items then in the news. He even sent me a book called *The Language of Food* to inspire me. Also, friendship had been a theme of Steve's shows since *Company*, and this show fit into his corpus like tongue-and-groove.

Exactly how and when we first discussed the Buñuel idea, and how and when we secured the film rights, are a bit vague. But Steve and I must have launched into work right on top of our old project. My last *All Together Now* notes and my first Buñuel notes are both dated August, 2013. We watched the two Buñuel films together at Steve's house one evening and started brainstorming. In the beginning – in fact, for a year – we planned to set the entire show in France. Paris is the quintessential bourgeois city, and the lightness of the film in the hands of Delphine Seyrig, Jean-Pierre Cassel and Stéphane Audran made us want to capture their effortless air of inborn Gallic entitlement. France might also take some of the curse off the social status of our main characters.

'Who wants to hear about *the rich*?' Steve said. 'Unless they're French?'

In the end we changed our minds, realizing that France didn't make the show lighter, France made it feel irrelevant. This had to be an American musical on American themes with American characters. It all came together quickly. Within a year we had an outline of pretty much the whole thing.

Then we found out that the hot young English composer Thomas Adès was working on an opera of *The Exterminating Angel* that was scheduled to be performed at the Salzburg Festival in 2016. Agents and estates were called in. Ultimately, both projects went forward because Adès planned a fairly faithful rendering of Buñuel's film while we were 'adapting' it. Steve and I went to see the Adès opera together when it came to the Met in 2017 and this time he didn't feel foxed. We continued work.

A title for the show eluded us for a long time. Mostly we just referred to it as 'Buñuel'. Sometimes I suggested we simply call it that and let people figure it out. Here's a partial list of titles we considered:

A Perfect Day
I Like It Right Here
It Is What It Is
Everybody into the Car
Let's Eat
Bon Appetit
Live It Up
The Specials
Din-Din
Dinner is Served

Piece of Cake
Square One
If It Isn't the War, It's the Weather
Here We Are
Life Goes On
What's Up?
Charmed Circle
Burger Deluxe
Café Everything
The Commonwealth
What the Hell

Late in the process, Steve caused some confusion by going on *The Late Show* and telling Stephen Colbert on national television that the title of the piece he was working on was *Square One*. That was in fact a working title, or the favorite working title of that week. The *Times* then complicated matters by running a couple of stories about the show that were short on true facts and seemed to have been fact-checked via Twitter. But this was all in the future. We were in the midst of work.

Contrary to his professed habit and his supposed 'German mind', Steve started writing music for the show before we'd settled on the details of the structure. First, he wrote a vamp for the top of the show. He then took the sequence in the movie where two of the characters have sex while their friends are waiting, and wrote what we called 'the fucking scene'. It was a farce number, with the copulating couple throwing off their clothes and getting it on while, in another part of the stage, the waiting friends make chit-chat. The number was funny but didn't move things forward, so we cut it.

In 2016, Joe Mantello joined the project as director. Joe is, of course, an electric actor onstage. As a director, he's a conjurer who at that point had already shown the wizardry he could bring to Sondheim material in his great production of *Assassins* – one of the greatest evenings of the theatre I've ever experienced. Taut, honest, fiercely principled and tireless, Joe quickly saw ways to focus the material – and ran straight into Steve's procrastination. Joe was no more successful than I'd been in getting him to turn out new musical material. Along the way, at Steve's suggestion, Alexander Gemignani joined us as musical director.

Unfortunately, just to complicate matters, I was losing interest in the theatre. I'd been writing plays since high school and college, and after forty years' work had grown immune to theatre's charms somewhat the way Mithridates became immune to poison: through extended intentional exposure. I gradually stopped going to shows, gave up my position on the Dramatists Guild Council and my Tony tickets, stopped reading theatre reviews, stopped following theatre news, didn't care what was on. The social side of theatre – openings, galas, award ceremonies and lunches – had never held much interest for me in any case. Given all this, plus Steve's dilatoriness, it seemed time for me to retire from the project.

I suggested to Steve he find another bookwriter to work with, someone who could finish what I'd begun and who might inspire him to finish the score. Our friendship remained intact while he approached other writers. Apparently a brief collaboration with a British bookwriter didn't work out. He came back to me, asked if I'd be willing to try again, and I rejoined him on the project.

The beginnings of macular degeneration overtook procrastination and gave Steve a serious excuse for not being able to produce music quickly. At this point, I had been working with Steve long enough that one of his two black poodles, young when we'd begun, had to be put down because of age and illness. Steve had always talked openly and eloquently and sometimes hilariously about old age. He once said to me that, given Donald Trump and approaching climate catastrophes, 'It's not a bad time to be leaving the world.' After Covid struck I didn't see much of Steve in person because he moved pretty much full-time to his house in Connecticut with his husband, Jeff Romley. Steve and I continued to talk on the phone all the time, though Albert Bassermann and Linda Darnell and Frank McHugh took up far more of our conversation time than Luis Buñuel.

By the spring of 2021, Steve seemed to have completely stalled on the Buñuel score. He had written numbers up to the point where the guests in Act Two realize they're 'trapped' in the room. Then one day Joe called me up. Looking at the script afresh, he'd had an epiphany: in terms of the score, the show was finished exactly as it stood. He said it was *right* that the music stopped where it did. Small wonder Steve had bogged down: those characters trapped in a room *had no reason to sing*. One of Steve's principles, expressed again and again in his two volumes of lyrics, was 'Content dictates form.' Without us realizing it, our show had found its proper form. There was music up to a certain logical point, and little or no music after that except for underscoring.

Joe suggested that he and I approach Steve and ask permission to sharpen up the book on our own. Steve wouldn't have to write another note. Steve heard us out and gave us the go-ahead. I warned him that we might have to disrupt some of his own writing in the course of our re-do.

Steve was fine with that. 'Disrupt,' he said.

Joe and I then spent six weeks in intense collaboration. Every day I'd email my rewrites to Joe in California and we'd go over them on the phone, line by line and word by word, in intense, sometimes hours-long conversations. One day, lacking earbuds but needing to listen to Joe's notes while I typed, I gorilla-taped my iPhone to a baseball cap and entered changes onto my screen wearing my cellphone hanging off the side of my head like half of a half-pound set of earmuffs.

In late summer we showed Steve what we'd done and he liked it. As things turned out, we hadn't needed to disrupt much of what Steve had written – two lines, as I recall, with his approval. Joe set up a closed reading, without music, in September 2021 so that Steve could hear what we had.

The last time I saw Sondheim in person was at that reading. It took place in a rented room at the LGBTQ+ Center in the West Village, with Nathan Lane and Bernadette Peters taking the leads. It was a roomful of theatre experts and luminaries, some of whom, like Bernadette, had long history with Sondheim. None of them had committed to the project. They were there for Steve. When I arrived that morning, Steve was already in the room, sitting at the table chatting with Nathan. Though Steve was walking with a cane, he looked spry and seemed in excellent spirits. Joe called the room to order, the actors read, Steve scribbled down some notes, then he said goodbye to the players and hung around to give Joe and me his thoughts.

He agreed with Joe. The show had integrity exactly as it stood. Though there were still loose ends, the kinds of things a musical director could do, underscoring that Steve could write himself or oversee, fundamentally Steve's work was done. He gave us the nod. The show should go up. Shortly thereafter, he gave the same nod to Rick Pappas, his lawyer and future executor. Without that crucial approval, the show could never have gone up.

I walked Steve out of the building that afternoon. He wasn't running out to hail a cab, as he had been at our first meeting a dozen years before. This time, a driver was waiting at the curb with a long black Town car. Steve had left his Covid mask behind in the room, so I gave him the spare I carried. We talked for a moment at the curb, the driver opened the door of the long black Town car and, wearing my mask, Sondheim got in the car and rode off literally into the sunset along West 13th Street. Two months later, he died at his home in Connecticut on Thanksgiving evening. Steve would have loved the irony, given the show he'd been working on for eight years. He passed away, after a dinner with friends, on a holiday that's all about food, on a day when everyone in the country – just like our cast of characters – is out for a meal.

The production process kicked in. Producers took on the project, the brilliant Sam Pinkleton signed on as choreographer, David Zinn and Natasha Katz and Tom Gibbons came on as, respectively, set/costume, lighting and sound designers, Jonathan Tunick joined us as orchestrator, Alex Gemignani continued as musical director. We held auditions over several weeks of spring 2023, in person in town and also (one of the horrors of contemporary theatre) via tape. In midsummer, Joe and I spent hours in conversation over a couple of days with culture critic Frank Rich, leading to a long piece in *New York Magazine*'s Fall Preview issue chronicling the gestation and development of the show. Our producers had wisely decided that that article would be the sole pre-press on our show. Rehearsals began in late summer for an October opening.

Rumors and opinions and misinformation about the show flew – rumors and opinions floated all too often by people who had nothing to do with the show, who hadn't attended any of the workshops or so much as been in the same room as a script. One erstwhile and now irrelevant producer who'd had nothing whatsoever to do with it said in the press that Steve had told him shortly before his death that the show wasn't finished. *Of course* the show was unfinished at that point: there were those musical transitions to be written, instrumentation to be added, tweaks and changes to be made during previews. No show is ever 'finished' until opening night, and Steve knew that.

Given such coverage, along with the rumor and opinion mill of social media and chat rooms, one would have thought that everyone involved in the show was trying to put something over on the public instead of doing what we were doing, which is to say bringing theatre audiences, always hungry for more Sondheim, more Sondheim. These were music and lyrics that nobody out there had ever heard. So we weren't supposed to finish the platform they'd been created for? We shouldn't show people what had been on the mind of a great American artist for his last eight years?

Joe and I kept our heads down and continued to do our job: finishing this particular and peculiar hat. In the end, the Buñuel project, now titled *Here We Are*, opened at The Shed on West 30th Street in New York City on October 22, 2023, to packed, cheering houses.

Finished indeed.

*

> We learn in the Retreating
> How vast an one
> Was recently among us –
> A Perished Sun.

Emily Dickinson

In science there are things called hyperobjects, entities so big and so complex that they defy easy comprehension. The sea is one. The sun is another. Black holes, capitalism, climate change and Shakespeare all qualify. Sondheim was – and remains – a theatrical hyperobject. He spent a long, rich lifetime composing scores for unlikely and often critically derided projects that became essential American masterpieces. *Sweeney Todd* is our *Hamlet*, *Into the Woods* our *Midsummer Night's Dream*, *Assassins* our *Macbeth*, *Follies* our *King Lear*. Though he wrote each of those wildly diverse shows with a different collaborator, each of them remains recognizably Sondheim: as precise as a van Eyck, as vivid as a Hockney, as witty and worldly as Wilde. It's hard to think of another theatre artist since Shakespeare working in English who so fully chronicled his times and the human world while putting himself – and his Inner Selves – so thoroughly on view. And there he was, in our midst, a theatrical genius who, like the sun and the sea and Shakespeare, managed simultaneously to be totally present and available and yet at the same time somehow hidden, mysterious.

I've begun to dream about Steve again, though the dreams aren't usually about invitations to his house. Recently I dreamt that I and a group of actors were putting up Steve's 'last work'. In the midst of rehearsal, Steve walked out onto the stage. We all knew that he was dead but we gathered around him, greeting him, glad to have him back. He looked good, seemed cheerful – and sat down at the director's table. I sat down next to him. The lights changed. Actors took their places. We got to work.

Needless to say, I miss my friend and our amazing afternoons. I miss the talk, the dish, the late-night phone calls, the Margaret Sullavan imitation and the story about mixing a martini for Princess Margaret when he didn't know how to make one. I miss the sudden erupting laugh, the equally sudden and surprising tears. I miss that unmistakable, resonant voice showing up on my voicemail saying, '*Hello, this is George Gershwin.*' And then, in his Jewish-mother voice, 'You never *write*, you never *call*…'

As George Bernard Shaw said at a friend's funeral, you don't lose a man like that by his death. You only lose him by your own.

Here We Are received its world premiere at The Shed, New York City, on 22 October 2023 (previews from 28 September). The cast (in alphabetical order) was as follows:

COLONEL MARTIN	Francois Battiste
WOMAN	Tracie Bennett
LEO BRINK	Bobby Cannavale
FRITZ	Micaela Diamond
CLAUDIA BURSIK-ZIMMER	Amber Gray
SOLDIER	Jin Ha
MARIANNE BRINK	Rachel Bay Jones
MAN	Denis O'Hare
RAFFAEL SANTELLO DI SANTICCI	Steven Pasquale
BISHOP	David Hyde Pierce
PAUL ZIMMER	Jeremy Shamos
A VISITOR	Adante Carter

Understudies

COLONEL MARTIN/LEO BRINK/ RAFFAEL SANTELLO DI SANTICCI	Bradley Dean
WOMAN/ CLAUDIA BURSIK-ZIMMER	Lindsay Nicole Chambers and Mehry Eslaminia
FRITZ/MARIANNE BRINK	Mehry Eslaminia and Bligh Voth
SOLDIER	Adante Carter
MAN/BISHOP/PAUL ZIMMER	Adam Harrington

Orchestra

Conductor/Associate Music Supervisor	Meghann Zervoulis Bate
Associate Conductor/Keyboards	Justin Hornback
Reeds	Jim Ercole, Lino Gomez, Patricia Wang and Keve Wilson

Trumpet	Hugo Moreno
Horn	Priscilla Rinehart
Drums/Percussion	Matt Smallcomb
Violins	Cenovia Cummins and Rachel Handman
Viola	Orlando Wells
Cello	Caryl Paisner
Bass	Matt Aronoff
Synthesizer Programming	Randy Cohen, Randy Cohen Keyboard LLC
Music Coordinator	Kimberlee Wertz
Music Copying	Katharine Edmonds, Alden Terry, Emily Grishman Music Preparation
Director	Joe Mantello
Scenic and Costume Design	David Zinn
Choreography	Sam Pinkleton
Orchestrations	Jonathan Tunick
Music Supervision and Additional Arrangements	Alexander Gemignani
Lighting Design	Natasha Katz
Sound Design	Tom Gibbons
Hair and Make-up Design	Robert Pickens and Katie Gell
Casting	Bernard Telsey CSA and Adam Caldwell CSA
General Manager	Megan Curren
Company Manager	Celina Lam
Production Stage Manager	William Joseph Barnes
Stage Manager	Luke Anderson
Assistant Stage Managers	Alex Eberle and Adriana Guerrero
Music Coordination	Kimberlee Wertz
Production Manager	Juniper Street Productions
Press Representative	DKC/O&M
Associate Director	Trey Ellett
Associate Choreographer	Billy Bustamante

Associate Music Supervisor   Meghann Zervoulis Bate
Associate Producer   Oscar Arce

Here We Are was originally produced by
Tom Kirdahy, Sue Wagner, John Johnson, The Stephen Sondheim Trust
Hunter Arnold, John Gore, Marguerite Hoffman, Peter May, Ted Snowdon, Steven Spielberg and Kate Capshaw
Caiola Productions, Concord Theatricals, Suzi Dietz and Lenny Beer, Hunter Johnson, Ken and Mady Kades, Willette and Manny Klausner, Viajes Miranda, Thomas M. Neff, Jillian Robbins, Kevin Ryan, The Shubert Organization, Wild Oak Media, 895 Broadway Partners
Josephine Bearden, Heni Koenigsberg/Cynthia J. Tong, InStone Productions/George Strus and The Shed

Here We Are was originally developed at the Public Theater, New York City (Oskar Eustis, Artistic Director; Patrick Willingham, Executive Director).

Here We Are received its UK premiere in the Lyttelton Theatre at the National Theatre, London, on 8 May 2025 (previews from 25 April). The cast (in alphabetical order) was as follows:

WOMAN	Tracie Bennett
A VISITOR/ENSEMBLE	Jack Butterworth
FRITZ	Chumisa Dornford-May
PAUL ZIMMER	Jesse Tyler Ferguson
SOLDIER	Richard Fleeshman
BISHOP	Harry Hadden-Paton
COLONEL MARTIN	Cameron Johnson
LEO BRINK	Rory Kinnear
MARIANNE BRINK	Jane Krakowski
MAN	Denis O'Hare
CLAUDIA BURSIK-ZIMMER	Martha Plimpton
RAFFAEL SANTELLO DI SANTICCI	Paulo Szot
ENSEMBLE	Edward Baker-Duly, Alastair Brookshaw, Molly Lynch, Amira Matthews, Steven Serlin

Understudies

WOMAN/CLAUDIA BURSIK-ZIMMER	Amira Matthews
A VISITOR/COLONEL MARTIN/ RAFFAEL SANTELLO DI SANTICCI	Steven Serlin
FRITZ/MARIANNE BRINK	Molly Lynch
PAUL ZIMMER/BISHOP	Alastair Brookshaw
SOLDIER	Jack Butterworth
LEO BRINK/MAN	Edward Baker-Duly

Orchestra

Conductor	Nigel Lilley
Associate Conductor/Keyboard	Cat Beveridge

Upright Bass	Marcus Pritchard
Kit/Percussion	Matt French
Trumpet	Angela Whelan
French Horn	Anna Douglass
Woodwind 1: Piccolo/Flute/Clarinet	James Mainwaring
Woodwind 2: Oboe/Cor Anglais	Maisie Ireland
Woodwind 3: Clarinet/Bass Clarinet/ Alto Saxophone	Dan Czwartos
Woodwind 4: Bassoon	Lully Bathurst
Violin 1 (Leader)	Tom Pigott-Smith
Violin 2	Naoko Keatley
Viola	Tina Jacobs-Lim
Cello	Dom Pecheur
Director	Joe Mantello
Set and Costume Designer	David Zinn
Choreographer	Sam Pinkleton
Orchestrations	Jonathan Tunick
Additional Arrangements	Alexander Gemignani
UK Music Supervisor and Conductor	Nigel Lilley
Lighting Designer	Natasha Katz
Sound Designer	Tom Gibbons
Wigs, Hair and Make-up Designers	Robert Pickens and Katie Gell
Casting	Bryony Jarvis-Taylor CDG
Original US Casting	The Telsey Office
Dialect Coach	Caitlin Stegemoller
Associate Director	Lily Dyble
Associate Set Designer	Tim McMath
Associate Costume Designer	Rachael Ryan
Associate Choreographer	Billy Bustamante
Associate Conductor	Cat Beveridge
Associate Lighting Designer	Craig Stelzenmuller
Associate Sound Designer	James Melling

A Tom Kirdahy, Sue Wagner, John Johnson and The Stephen Sondheim Trust production
Co-produced with the National Theatre
In association with Thomas M. Neff, Steven Spielberg and Kate Capshaw

HERE WE ARE

David Ives and Stephen Sondheim

Characters

in order of appearance

LEO BRINK
MARIANNE BRINK
FRITZ
PAUL ZIMMER
CLAUDIA BURSIK-ZIMMER
RAFFAEL SANTELLO DI SANTICCI
EVA
MAITRESSE D'
WAITER
FRENCH WAITRESS
ITALIAN WAITER
COLONEL MARTIN
SOLDIER
SOLDIER'S MOTHER
WINDSOR
McGOGG
BISHOP
A VISITOR

This text went to press before the end of rehearsals and so may differ slightly from the play as performed.

ACT ONE: THE ROAD

Scene One

MARIANNE AND LEO'S APARTMENT, Saturday morning.

LIGHTS UP on a luxury apartment high over a city. Present are:

LEO BRINK, *sixties, bullet-shaped and energetic, in top-dollar sweatpants, sweatshirt and Topsiders.*

MARIANNE BRINK, *late thirties, a willowy beauty in an expensive peignoir and satin slippers.*

MARIANNE's *sister* FRITZ, *twenty-nine, scruffy and self-starved in East Village cast-offs, snapping pictures with a camera.*

PAUL ZIMMER, *forty, laid back, with bland good looks.*

CLAUDIA BURSIK-ZIMMER, *early forties, sexy; both she and* PAUL *are in pricey informal wear.*

RAFFAEL SANTELLO DI SANTICCI, *fifty, cosmopolitan and suave, in a white suit with medals and an ambassadorial sash, carrying flowers.*

EVA, *a gloomy Polish maid.*

MARIANNE. O, isn't this *wonderful*?!

LEO. Marianne was just saying –

MARIANNE. I was just saying to Leo, we haven't seen Paul and Claudia for *ages*!

LEO. Then the doorbell rings!

MARIANNE. And now here's the whole gang! Raffael!

RAFFAEL. Oh, la bellellita Marianita!

> RAFFAEL *gives her flowers.* MARIANNE *hands the flowers to* EVA, *and* MARIANNE *and* RAFFAEL *embrace.*

CLAUDIA. You shoulda seen the madhouse getting here.

MARIANNE (*embracing her sister*). O, and my little Frit*zie*!

PAUL. We get this Polynesian cabbie who only speaks *Korean*.

CLAUDIA. Or something.

FRITZ. Yeah, who you totally stiffed. (*Pulling free of* MARIANNE*'s embrace.*) And I told you, it's Fritz. Okay?

MARIANNE. I'm sorry, Fritzie. I keep forgetting!

CLAUDIA. Then your schmuck doorman says, 'Are you *expected*.'

PAUL. And did Claudia read this guy the riot act?! Whoa!

CLAUDIA. I said, 'We're their closest friends, and this is Raffael di San Blah-Blah, the ambassador of *Moranda*.'

PAUL. And then she says –

CLAUDIA. 'I represent a major entertainment entity. Send us up or I sue this fucking building.'

RAFFAEL. Then your enchanting sister critiques capitalism for ninety stories.

LEO. No! Not Frit*zie*.

FRITZ (*with their usual bantering edge*). *Good morning, Leo*.

PAUL. Anyway, taa-daaa! We made it!

THE GUESTS (FRITZ *joining in, deadpan*). Hurray!

LEO. Terrific, great! So why are you here?

PAUL. Why are we *here*? Bring on the omelettes!

CLAUDIA. And coffee, please! Immediately!

MARIANNE. You mean – you're *supposed* to be here?

CLAUDIA. Well, *brunch*, remember?

LEO. Today?

CLAUDIA. Saturday! You *invited* us, Leo.

RAFFAEL. To your paradise apartment!

ACT ONE: THE ROAD   5

MARIANNE. Eva? Was there a brunch today?

EVA (*Polish accent*). Mad-dam, I am in complete mystery.

FRITZ. Oh, this is classic! Smile!

FRITZ snaps a picture of the group with the camera.

LEO. I musta had some kinda brain fart! Me? Forget a *brunch*?

MARIANNE. Isn't this *awful*? But also sort of funny! (*To* EVA.) Eva – (*To* LEO.) Darling, do you think? – Eva, could you scramble some eggs for one, two, three…

EVA. *Mad-DAM*. Nothing is prepared. Cook is off. I have headache. *NO!*

EVA thrusts the FLOWERS back in RAFFAEL's hands and EXITS.

CLAUDIA. Paul, did we screw this up or did *you* screw this up?

PAUL. Saturday! It's in my phone, sweetie!

CLAUDIA. It's not in *my* phone, sweetie.

THEY hold up dueling phones as proof and air-kiss. ALL stop for:

MARIANNE. Wait a minute, wait a minute! There *was* something I was supposed to do today! Something very important. Let me see, Treadmill? Manicure? Zumba class…?

Simultaneous:

MARIANNE. No, really, it's something important!
CLAUDIA. I'm *starving*, that's what's important!
FRITZ. You were supposed to be a *caring human being*!
PAUL. You have *brunch* today, that's what you have!
RAFFAEL. What could you possibly have on a Saturday?
LEO. Hold it, hold it, hold it!

RAFFAEL. No, no, listen! Mimis amichichis! Today, just to be with you all… (*Taking* CLAUDIA *and* MARIANNE *around the waist.*) …and with beautiful women? *This* is important!

LEO. Raffi's right. Who gives a fuck whose fault it was!

PAUL. Hear, hear!

LEO. So, kids – I'm taking us all to brunch!

THE GROUP (FRITZ *joining in, deadpan*). Yay!

CLAUDIA. I want my coffee!

PAUL. I want some protein!

LEO. You know what I want? *Nothing.* Nothing, nothing, nothing – except us who are here in this room.

CLAUDIA. *And* some coffee.

LEO. And coffee and protein and blah blah blah. Besides that? Sweet fuck-all! *NOTHIN'!*

MARIANNE. Isn't he the sweetest thing? (*Kisses the top of LEO's head.*) I'll go change.

RAFFAEL. No, no, no you look ravishing, you must come as you are!

RAFFAEL *hands her a WHITE ROSE from the bouquet.*

MARIANNE. In my negligee?

LEO. You think any restaurant's gonna turn away Leo Brink? (*Calls offstage.*) *Charlie!* (*To them.*) We could wear *jockstraps*, they'd feed us.

FRITZ. Wow, that's real power, Leo.

CHARLES *ENTERS, a liveried chauffeur.*

CHARLES. Yes, Mr Brink?

LEO. Charlie, bring the car around, will you.

CHARLES *EXITS.* FRITZ *is snapping pictures.*

MARIANNE. Fritzie, what are you doing?

FRITZ. I'm documenting the end of civilization.

MARIANNE. Yes, but *today*?

LEO. Screw civilization. Who's hungry, anybody hungry?

CLAUDIA. Starving.

ACT ONE: THE ROAD 7

RAFFAEL. Ravenous.

PAUL. Totally famished.

LEO. Well then, let's find some food! Everybody into the car!

The SCENE CHANGES, rather unexpectedly, to…

Road 1

A pleasant road amid vast, featureless fields in early morning spring sunshine. We hear the occasional CHATTER of BIRDS. Our group starts walking in place with the country landscape on view around them. This is 'the car'.

A MUSICAL VAMP. The DIALOGUE becomes RHYTHMIC.

LEO. All right, where do we wanna eat?

PAUL. Anything but Mexican.

RAFFAEL. Why, what's wrong with Mexican?

PAUL. It's too spicy.

CLAUDIA. It's too cheese-y.

PAUL. And it always looks pre-eaten.

They laugh.

MARIANNE. But what was it I was supposed to *do* today? No matter!

MARIANNE sniffs the white rose she's carrying.

(*Sings, echoing the melody.*) What a perfect day!
  On a day like today,
  What could ever go wrong?

LEO. Okay, 'No' to Mexican, then how about Italian?

PAUL. North Italian.

RAFFAEL (*disdainfully*). 'North Italian'…

CLAUDIA. He means Tuscan. (*To* PAUL.) Don't you, lovey.

PAUL. I mean North Italian. (*Firmly.*) Venetian.

PAUL *and* CLAUDIA *exchange air kisses.*

MARIANNE. What if we try this new place, Café Everything?

CLAUDIA. It got great reviews.

LEO. Then I say, hell yes!

THE GROUP walks in silence for a moment.

MARIANNE. You look wistful, Dr. Zimmer.

PAUL. I had a big milestone this week. My one thousandth nose job.

MARIANNE. Congratulations!

LEO. Anybody we know?

LIGHTS CHANGE abruptly and the MUSIC becomes an intense TANGO as RAFFAEL swoops CLAUDIA up and dances with her briefly. The OTHERS remain oblivious of them.

RAFFAEL (*sotto voce*). I have to have you…

CLAUDIA (*sotto voce*). I know…

MARIANNE (*sings*).
  Face it, are we not blessed!

LIGHTS go back to normal and the VAMP resumes. RAFFAEL and CLAUDIA break apart and rejoin the group.

  If it isn't the sun, it's the birdsong.
  If it isn't the air, it's the view.

CLAUDIA*'s PHONE rings. As* MARIANNE *continues,* CLAUDIA *looks with annoyance at the caller's name but takes the call.*

  I'm completely undone
  By the endless abundance of life,
  Aren't you?

CLAUDIA (*barking into her phone*). Yes, what?!

MARIANNE (*sings*).
  Don't we all feel blessed!

FRITZ *rolls her eyes and grunts with disgust.* MARIANNE, *with a tight smile, raises her fingers in admonition not to say anything.* FRITZ *takes a picture of it. Simultaneously:*

CLAUDIA (*into phone, speaks*). Tell ABC to screw themselves!

MARIANNE (*sings*).
 Blessed with health –

CLAUDIA *shuts her PHONE and smiles sunnily at the others.*

 Blessed with friends –

RAFFAEL.
 Blessed with Shakespeare –

PAUL.
 Teslas –

CLAUDIA.
 Honey –

LEO (*leering clownishly at* MARIANNE).
 Blessed with boobies –

MARIANNE (*pokes him affectionately, speaks*). Very funny.

FRITZ (*sings*).
 Blessed with tons and tons of –

CLAUDIA (*wearily, speaks*). We get it, Fritzie.

FRITZ (*irritated, speaks*). Fritz.

CLAUDIA. Sorry. (*To* MARIANNE.) Remember when she was 'Frances'?

MARIANNE. O, how I miss those days.

 PAUL *has sidled over to* RAFFAEL.

PAUL (*sotto voce*). (Is there any news from 'Abdul'?)

 CLAUDIA*'s PHONE rings.*

RAFFAEL (*sotto voce*). (Not now.)

CLAUDIA (*to herself, snapping her phone open*). Now what?

PAUL (*alarmed, to* RAFFAEL). (What's wrong?)

RAFFAEL *shrugs noncommittally.*

MARIANNE. That sky – !

CLAUDIA (*into the phone*). What now?!

PAUL (*alarmed to* RAFFAEL). (Are there problems with the shipment?)

RAFFAEL. (Could be.)

CLAUDIA (*into the phone*). Fat chance!

MARIANNE. What luck!

PAUL. (What if – ?)

RAFFAEL *looks over to* LEO *for help.*

MARIANNE. Such bliss – !

LEO (*to* PAUL). (Will you relax?)

MARIANNE (*sings to* LEO, *flinging her arms wide*).
    Buy this day for me, darling,
    Buy this perfect day
    Put it on display,
    Let it stay
    Just this way
    Forever.

MARIANNE *waves the others to join in.* FRITZ *ignores her.* CLAUDIA *stays on the phone.*

MARIANNE / PAUL / RAFFAEL.
    Yes, buy this day for us, Leo,
    Buy this perfect day.

MARIANNE *waves* CLAUDIA *to get off the phone.*

CLAUDIA (*sito phone, sotto voce*). Hold on…

MARIANNE / PAUL / CLAUDIA / RAFFAEL.
    Keep it on display,
    Let it stay
    Just this way
    Forever.

LIGHTS CHANGE and the TANGO re-enters underneath. RAFFAEL grabs MARIANNE and swoops her around. As before, the OTHERS, oblivious of RAFFAEL and MARIANNE, keep walking.

CLAUDIA (*into phone*). Go ahead…

MARIANNE. I found you a credenza for your Embassy.

RAFFAEL (*sotto voce, to* MARIANNE). Never mind credenzas.

MARIANNE. And a vintage Aubusson that's darling.

RAFFAEL. *Darling* – I have to have you…

MARIANNE (*glancing nervously around*). Raffi, what are you saying – ?

RAFFAEL. I'm saying I have to have you. 'La vidida ay estada el tidada'! (*As* MARIANNE *nods uncomprehendingly:*) It's an old Morandan proverb.

MARIANNE (*putting him off*). Well, it's lovely.

RAFFAEL (*murmuring flirtatiously*). 'La vidida –'

MARIANNE (*shouting to the others*). Listen, everybody – !

EVERYONE stops talking.

(*To* RAFFAEL.) Say it, Raffi, once again. (*Waving her hands excitedly.*) Listen, people!

THEY slow down a bit to listen, but keep walking.

RAFFAEL. 'La vidida ay estada el tidada.'

MARIANNE. Don't you love it? (*With hyper-elegant pronunciation.*) 'La vidida ay estada el tidada.'

RAFFAEL *nods approvingly.*

PAUL (*snapping his fingers, mock-Mexican*). 'La vidida ay estada el tidada.'

PAUL *conducts the others, who dance around as they chant.* FRITZ *does not join in.*

ALL (*EXCEPT* FRITZ). La vidida ay estada el tidada!

MARIANNE (*gesturing poetically*). It just flows…

ALL (*EXCEPT* FRITZ). La vidida ay estada el tidada!

CLAUDIA. Meaning what?

RAFFAEL. 'Life's a tit!' (*As* MARIANNE *looks startled:*) 'Suck it up!'

EVERYBODY except FRITZ laughs. MUSIC resumes.

ALL (*EXCEPT* FRITZ). La vidida ay estada el tidada!
La vidida ay estada el tidada!
La vidida ay estada el tidada!

FRITZ. Jesus Christ…

MARIANNE (*impatiently, to* FRITZ). Now what?

FRITZ. Now what?!

An OUTBURST of MUSIC from the ORCHESTRA.

(*Sings, explosively.*)
Only just the end of the world,
That's what!
Nothing but the end of the world!
Comes the revolution –
Don't laugh! It's coming!
Can't you hear the sound of that distant drumming?
Once the revolution is up and humming,
That'll be the end of the world,
Your world:
The world of private jets and screening rooms
And hundred-thousand-bucks-an-ounce designer
   perfumes,
The world of Wall Street thieves and fashionistas
And Lamborghinis and Vodkatinis –
It's all so over! Don't you know that?

RAFFAEL. Oh, Fritz – a little joy, per favavere! Life is pleasure! We have this day. We have our charmful circle!

MARIANNE. You mean charmed.

RAFFAEL. It's my English… But why not? Call us charmful!
And rejoice, Fritz, rejoice!

ACT ONE: THE ROAD   13

FRITZ.
>Wake up, it's the end of the world,
>You morons,
>Welcome to the end of
>Power brokers and hydrofractors
>And underpaid teachers and overpaid actors
>And disappearing polar bears
>And bought-and-sold elections
>And infinity pools
>And Damien Hirsts
>And phony bank accounts –
>With safe-deposit boxes in
>Corrupt banana rat-holes
>Like Moranda!
>They're gonna blow your mergers
>And your laptops
>And your bitcoins
>All to bits!

CLAUDIA (*softly, shaking her head warily*). Fritz…

MARIANNE. And abracadabra, here's Café Everything!

ALL (*EXCEPT* FRITZ). What a perfect day.

FRITZ. What a perfect day.

MUSIC stops. THE SCENE CHANGES to…

Scene Two: Café Everything

MARIANNE. Why, this place is perfectly *adorable*!

FRITZ *takes a picture of it. The* MAITRESSE D' *ENTERS.*

MAITRESSE D'. Good morning, eaters. Welcome to Café Everything. A celebration of plenitude, a hymn to abundance, a paean to endless plenty! Case in point – ? (*Presenting a MASSIVE BLACK BOOK:*) Our menu.

LEO. Amazing. Listen, we don't have a reservation…

MAITRESSE D'. Oh, please. Are you not *Leo Brink*? And – of course – Mrs Brink? And his excellency Señor-r-ro R-r-raffael Santello di Santicci, the Mor-r-randan ambassador? Along with... others, no doubt worthy? Of course we have a table for you. This way.

A TABLE APPEARS with only SIX MASSIVE BLACK-BOUND MENUS and SIX EMPTY WATER GLASSES on it.

Here we are. I hope this is acceptable. Your enabler will be here momentarily.

MARIANNE. '*Enabler.*' Is that delicious?

MAITRESSE D'. Enjoy.

CLAUDIA. Excuse me! Excuse me! Can I substitute?

MAITRESSE D'. At Café Everything? *Everything!*

THEY take seats. RAFFAEL slips himself between CLAUDIA and FRITZ.

MARIANNE. Could we have some water, please?

MAITRESSE D'. I will check on that.

PAUL. Wow. They really do have everything.

CLAUDIA. And then some.

LEO. Abalone omelettes with saffron...

RAFFAEL. Curried goat hash. I love a good goat!

MARIANNE. They've got manna? I'm in heaven!

LEO (*his PHONE BURPS and he takes it out*). That's me. (*Into phone.*) Leo Brink.

MARIANNE. Not at the table, darling.

LEO. Right. Sorry...

LEO goes aside to talk on his phone.

MARIANNE. Oh oh oh, did I tell you we're getting the dogs cloned?

PAUL. You're *what*?!

MARIANNE. We're getting the dogs cloned.

PAUL. Yeah, I heard. *You're cloning your dogs?*

MARIANNE. Isn't it *great*?

PAUL. Sure. I mean. Wow. But isn't that, for one thing, wildly expensive?

MARIANNE. It's worth it! Leo's tired of dragging them up to Connecticut, to Switzerland, to Boca. This way we'll have one set of dogs everywhere and they'll just be waiting for us.

PAUL. Which dogs will be the real dogs?

MARIANNE. They're all *real*. Even the copies!

LEO (*ending his phone call*). Order big, my friends. We're celebrating.

PAUL. My thousand nose jobs?

LEO. No, THE LEO BRINK PARK FOR THE PEOPLE! (*Shows them a TEXT on his phone.*) Just got the news.

ALL. *Yay!*

MARIANNE. Oh, darling, the City Council said yes?

LEO. To everything! The ferris wheel – bigger than London. The white shark and piranha tank. The virgin forest imported from Lithuania. All free to the people!

ALL applaud except FRITZ.

MARIANNE. I love it!

FRITZ. Leo. Ripping out A VIRGIN FOREST? Has anybody here ever heard of karma?

MARIANNE. They have karma here?!

FRITZ. They have it everywhere.

LEO. Fritzie, *it's not your money.*

FRITZ. It's the People's money.

LEO. Well, I have it for now.

FRITZ. Not for long you don't. They're coming for it.

LEO. Oh my God, no! *The People are coming!* THE PEOPLE ARE COMING! What'll I do?! (*Fake heart attack.*) GAAAAAAAAHHHHHH!

MARIANNE. Leo…

LEO. GAAAAAAAHHHHHHH!

FRITZ. Ha, ha.

LEO. Just cut the revolution crap, kiddo. You're here with us, you been coopted by the plutocracy, *enjoy yourself.*

PAUL. That settles it. I'm definitely having the karma.

All laugh but FRITZ. LEO *taps his empty water glass. CHORD.*

LEO (*sings*).
　Ladies and gents,
　Before we munch –

THEY ALL raise their empty glasses, except FRITZ.

　We must thank the Lord
　For inventing brunch –

CLAUDIA.
　For sourdough –

RAFFAEL.
　Petite Marmite –

PAUL.
　Good health –

MARIANNE.
　Good friends –

LEO (*pronouncing the final 't'*).
　Bon Appetit!

MARIANNE.
　Tee. Bon Appetee.

LEO.
　I know, I know.

　WAITER *ENTERS.*

WAITER. Good morning, adventurers! I'll be enabling your table.

PAUL. Do you have Malay duck?

WAITER. Sir. We're not called Café Everything for nothing.

MARIANNE. Could we have some water, please?

WAITER. I will check on that. Can I take your order?

CLAUDIA. Of course you *may*. It's your *job*.

THE OTHERS laugh. FRITZ groans out an embarrassed 'Eugh.'

I want a decaf soymilk latte mocchaniño. *Immediately.* (*Turns to the menu.*)

WAITER. Yes, ma'am!

CLAUDIA (*continuing to order*). And –

WAITER *EXITS*. CLAUDIA *looks up*.

That was literal.

MARIANNE. You said immediately.

CLAUDIA. I always say immediately.

PAUL. For everything.

CLAUDIA. I really am a very patient person.

WAITER *RE-ENTERS*.

Well?

MUSIC.

WAITER (*sings*).
 I am so sorry, Madam,
 We have no decaf latte mocchaniños
 With soy milk
 Today.

The dialogue throughout the following is in RHYTHM.

CLAUDIA (*impatiently*). Fine. Skip the soy.

WAITER (*apologetic*).
>   What can I say?

CLAUDIA. I said fine. Regular is f–

WAITER (*even more apologetic*)
>   That's not the problem, Madam.
>   The problem isn't just the soy,
>   You see,
>   It's more than just the soy.

CLAUDIA. Yeah, so – ?

WAITER.
>   I couldn't be more sorry, Madam,
>   But sad to say, the fact is
>   That not only do we have no soy –

PAUL. Oh, boy.

CLAUDIA. Don't tell me that you have no mocha –

WAITER (*overlapping*).
>   We have no mocha.

CLAUDIA. Then just a decaf latte, I don't –

WAITER (*overlapping*).
>   We're also out of latte.

CLAUDIA. What?!

WAITER.
>   We do expect a little latte later,
>   But we haven't got a lotta latte now.

RAFFAEL. You can't be out of latte – that would mean you're out of milk!

WAITER.
>   Sir, not only are we out of milk,
>   We're out of cream,
>   We're out of half-and-half.

CLAUDIA (*about to explode*). The caffe latte without the lat – !

WAITER.
>   We're also out of caf –

>   *Beat.*

CLAUDIA (*subdued, taken aback*). Not even 'de' – ?

WAITER. Is that a laugh?

HE shrugs helplessly.

CLAUDIA. All right then, tea. Twining's Earl Grey. Bag on the side.

WAITER. Ah… Yes… Well…

WAITER grimaces apologetically.

CLAUDIA. Don't tell me –

WAITER.
>I am so sorry, Madam,
>I do apologize,
>It's unforgivable,
>I'm so embarrassed,
>But not only are we out of Earl Grey,
>We're out of Earl Green,
>We're out of Earl Red and Blue
>And everything in between.

CLAUDIA. Okay then, Lipton's, I don't care, whatever –

WAITER (*overlapping*).
>I apologize profusely, Madam,
>But we're shit out of tea
>Today.

CLAUDIA. You've got to be kidding.

WAITER. Je suis désolé.

CLAUDIA (*in desperation*). Fine. Diet Coke with lem–

WAITER (*raises his hand*).
>Madam, if I may –
>I forgot to say,
>By the way,
>We have no Coke,
>We have no Sprite,
>We have no Mountain Dew,
>No Fresca Lite.
>And I should add, although I do regret it:
>If you're thinking beer or wine, forget it.

CLAUDIA. What is this? *Paraguay?* Do you have water?

MUSIC stops.

WAITER (*jotting it down*). I will check.

HE starts out. LEO *stops the* WAITER.

LEO. The hell with it. Let's just order. (*To* WAITER.) Gimme the abalone omelette, runny, extra saffron.

WAITER (*jotting it down*). Excellent choice.

MARIANNE. I've changed my mind about manna. I crave huevos rancheros.

WAITER. A superb selection.

MARIANNE. Mostly because I love the name. Huevoth rancheroth! Huevoth…!

CLAUDIA. *Marianne.* – I don't see it, have you got gluten-free beef?

WAITER. Madam, we're not called –

WAITER / CLAUDIA. – Café Everything for nothing.

CLAUDIA. Screw it, I'll do the blood pudding.

WAITER. How do you like your blood pudding?

CLAUDIA. Vampiric.

WAITER. *Nice.*

PAUL. Come back to me.

RAFFAEL. I will have the curried goat hash.

WAITER. Splendid.

PAUL. Do I *want* the Malay duck?

WAITER. It is an unparalleled experience.

PAUL. Done.

WAITER. And you – Sir, Madam or Mizzz, as the case may be?

FRITZ. First I want to apologize for my friends treating you like a servant.

WAITER. I am a servant. I am your servant. What can I bring you?

FRITZ. I'm gonna go basic. A cheeseburger. With blue cheese, medium. That's *California* medium, only pink around the edges. A lettuce wrap instead of a bun. Mustard, not ketchup. And sriracha, not Tabasco, sriracha –

LEO. *Just bring the shit, will you?* We're starving!

WAITER (*hesitantly*). Ah… Yes… well, perhaps I should have mentioned…

A beat, as THEY ALL look at him.

LEO. What.

MUSIC begins.

WAITER (*sings*).
 I am so sorry, sir, but
 We're out of abalone omelettes,
 Although I have to say they are delicious
 And I'm sure you'd like them if we had them
 But we don't.

LEO. Oh, for Christ's sake! (*Glances at the menu.*) Then make it two hashes, only make my goat medium –

WAITER.
 Nor have we any hash,
 Never mind the curried goat.
 And wait, I made a note:

Checks his pad.

 Oh yes, the huevos –

As MARIANNE *looks up hopefully.*

 Nada, sorry.
 Right, who had the duck?

PAUL *starts to raise his hand.*

 You're out of luck.

PAUL. Fuck.

WAITER.
>As for the –
>(*Winces.*) Ugh! Blood pudding –
>Well, I wouldn't recommend it anyway.

Simultaneous:

MARIANNE. This is ridiculous!
PAUL. Well, what do you have?
LEO. Why is it on the menu?
CLAUDIA. It's false advertising!
FRITZ. Will you all stop complaining?
RAFFAEL. I cannot eat in this condition!

The WAITER *raises his hands to quell the uproar.*

WAITER (*solemnly*).
 On behalf of the entire management and staff
 And international consortium
 That owns and operates Café Everything,
 (*Extremely penitent.*) I can't apologize enough,
 I just may go and kill myself.
 (*Becoming a big unhinged.*)
 That's what I'll do is kill myself.
 I'd rather kill myself
 Than have to tell you
 We're completely out of food!

CLAUDIA. How rude.

RAFFAEL. No – ?

He waves his hands ineffectually.

WAITER.
>Of any kind.

MARIANNE. Well, never mind.

WAITER.
>I should have given you some warning,
>But it's been a very busy morning.

CLAUDIA. Then why the hell did you take our orders?

WAITER. Madam, that's my *job*. I'll check on that water.

A FLOURISH of MUSIC and HE exits.

PAUL. I thought he wanted to kill himself.

LEO. Café *Nada*, they oughta call it.

CLAUDIA (*calls off toward* WAITER). *Hey!* Could you make that sparkling?

A GUNSHOT is heard. THE GROUP looks off, then at each other.

MARIANNE. What in the world was that?

LEO. Maybe a car backfiring.

PAUL. Yeah. That still happens.

FRITZ. No, it doesn't! That was a GUNSHOT.

CLAUDIA. Because I asked for *sparkling*?

FRITZ. You realize you may have killed an innocent waiter?

PAUL. What waiter is innocent? Really?

CLAUDIA. Why don't we go to Bistro À La Mode? It's French Deconstructivist cuisine.

MARIANNE. That sounds like fun! Sort of.

PAUL. We love it.

LEO. Well – back to square one. Everybody into the car!

THE SCENE CHANGES.

Road 2

MUSIC resumes, the familiar JAUNTY VAMP as THE GROUP resumes its 'ride', walking down what seems to be a country road.

CLAUDIA. So much for trying someplace new.

MARIANNE. What is happening to decent restaurants?

LEO (*sings*).
 If it isn't the food, it's the service.

FRITZ. Didn't you hear?

RAFFAEL.
>   If it isn't the noise, it's the queue.

FRITZ. Are you insane?!

PAUL.
>   Or the backs of the chairs –

LEO.
>   Or a waiter with airs –

CLAUDIA.
>   Or the long flight of stairs
>   To the loo.

MARIANNE.
>   There's always something…

The TANGO MUSIC suddenly begins. RAFFAEL *grabs* FRITZ.

RAFFAEL (*to* FRITZ, *sotto voce*). You know, you're hot when you are angry.

FRITZ. Forget it, Raffi. I've been gay since I was three.

A CELLPHONE RINGS. ALL reach for their phones.

Simultaneous:

PAUL. Is that mine?
LEO. Is it me?
CLAUDIA. That's me.

FRITZ. It's me, it's me, don't worry.

MARIANNE *grabs* FRITZ*'s phone from* FRITZ*'s hand.*

MARIANNE. A boyfriend, I hope!

FRITZ. Do you *mind*?

MARIANNE (*reading the caller*). '*PRADA*' calling?! Sweetheart, you told me you're anti-fashion!

FRITZ *grabs the PHONE back.*

FRITZ. Anti-*fascist*. Anti-*fascist*.

ACT ONE: THE ROAD 25

RAFFAEL. Did you know there's an extremist group of Lefties in Moranda who call themselves – would you believe it? PRADA.

FRITZ *moves away for privacy.*

FRITZ (*sotto voce, into phone*). (Apocalypse here.)

RAFFAEL. They communicate only in code.

FRITZ (*sotto voce, into phone*). (Yes, Inferno.)

RAFFAEL. Their leader is known only as 'Inferno'.

MARIANNE. And they're named after a shoe?

RAFFAEL. No, PRADA stands for 'People's' –

FRITZ (*sotto voce, into phone*). (Fifty *million*?!)

RAFFAEL. 'Revolutionary' –

FRITZ (*sotto voce, into phone*). (By tonight?!)

RAFFAEL. 'Anti-Domination' –

FRITZ (*sotto voce, into phone*). (*Why?*)

LEO. 'Assholes.'

RAFFAEL *laughs.*

PAUL. 'Assholes.' Really?

CLAUDIA *rolls her eyes.*

RAFFAEL. 'Army.'

FRITZ (*sotto voce, into phone*). (I know, I know, we can't delay the revolution…)

MARIANNE. Are they dangerous?

LEO. You ever meet an asshole who wasn't?

PAUL. Hey, *I'm* an asshole.

CLAUDIA. Yeah but, sweetie, you're not *dangerous*.

THEY air-kiss.

FRITZ (*sotto voce, into phone*). (Well, I do know a few rich assholes but they're not gonna hand over fifty million.)

TANGO MUSIC. RAFFAEL *sidles up to* CLAUDIA, *draws her aside and begins to DANCE with her.*

RAFFAEL (*sotto voce, to* CLAUDIA). I have to have you. *Now.*

CLAUDIA. How do you want me?

RAFFAEL. The way I had you last Tuesday…

CLAUDIA. I love that way.

RAFFAEL. I miss you every day –

CLAUDIA. Say it, say it – !

RAFFAEL. Every day –

FRITZ (*sotto voce, into phone*). (Okay, okay, okay.)

RAFFAEL (*sings*).
 In my heart,
 In my mind,
 In my bed –

CLAUDIA. More.

RAFFAEL.
 I miss the way you always give me
 Comfort, courage, head…

CLAUDIA. Bite me.

RAFFAEL (*pronouncing it 'Clowdia'*).
 Clowdia –
 I but murmur your name –

RAFFAEL*'S CELLPHONE RINGS and he breaks away from* CLAUDIA.

Excuse me.

FRITZ (*sotto voce, into phone*). (I'll do my best, Inferno.)

RAFFAEL (*sotto voce, into phone*). (Hello, Abdul.)

FRITZ (*raised fist*). (NADA BUT PRADA!)

FRITZ *hangs up her phone.*

Anybody want to donate fifty million bucks for a noble cause?

LEO. What's the cause?

FRITZ. The coming revolution.

MARIANNE. O, Fritzie, you are so *cute*!

LEO (*sings, jokingly, aimed at* FRITZ).
    What if it's the end of the world?
    Hey, folks,
    Maybe it's the end of the world!

FRITZ. Yeah, laugh…

  RAFFAEL *hangs up.*

RAFFAEL (*worried, partly to* PAUL, *partly to himself*). Maybe it's the end of the world, indeed…

MARIANNE (*overlapping*).
    In that case,
    (*To* LEO.) Buy this day for us, sweetheart,
    Buy this perfect day.

CLAUDIA. Agreed.

    End the world, okay,
    But this day,
    Let it stay!

PAUL.
    And as they say –

CLAUDIA.
    Paul.

PAUL (*snapping his fingers*)
    'La vidida ay estada el tidada!'

  (*Sexily, to* MARIANNE.) Olé…

    'La vidida ay estada el tidada!'

CLAUDIA. He needs food.

PAUL (*to the group*).
    'La vidida ay estada el tidada!'

  Right, Raffi?

MUSIC stops, but the DIALOGUE continues in RHYTHM.

RAFFAEL. Ordinarily, yes, life *is* a tit. (*Pointedly, to* PAUL *and* LEO.) *Today*, however...

PAUL *and* LEO *sidle over to him.* FRITZ *sees them.*

PAUL. What?

LEO. Yeah, 'however' *what*?

RAFFAEL. That was Abdul.

FRITZ *listens in.*

PAUL. Is it the diplomatic pouch? Did the Feds find the coke?

FRITZ. The *coke*? I love it.

FRITZ *takes out her PHONE and delightedly punches in numbers.*

RAFFAEL (*going into code, very loudly*). The *PUMPKINS*, yes, it seems the locusts have descended on the *pumpkins*.

PAUL. Oh my God.

RAFFAEL. We have to feed them lots of semolina.

PAUL. Jesus Christ!

LEO. There's a ton of semolina in the silo, so relax.

RAFFAEL. The *pumpkin* itself, however, is perfect!

RAFFAEL *quietly opens his POCKETWATCH and offers coke to LEO and PAUL. THEY take a pinch and sniff it.*

CLAUDIA (*to* MARIANNE). Did he just say locusts have descended on the pumpkins? What does that mean?

MARIANNE. It's poetry. Almost. And voilà, here's Bistro À La Mode!

LEO. Everybody out of the car!

FRITZ (*into her phone*). Hello, Inferno? That fifty mil is in the bag.

FRITZ *ends the call and THE SCENE CHANGES TO...*

Scene Three: Bistro À La Mode

The restaurant has A HEAVY RED VELVET CURTAIN in one corner.

MARIANNE. Why, this place is perfectly adorable! Sort of.

PAUL. Yeah, where is everybody?

RAFFAEL. No customers. Not a very good sign.

CLAUDIA. I'm telling you, you're going to love this place.

LEO. We just gotta get served first. Hello? *We're here and we're hungry!*

CLAUDIA. Usually Philippe comes out and greets us. (*Calling.*) *Bonjour!* Philippe?

A brief, low CHORD in the ORCHESTRA. A FEMALE VOICE is heard SOBBING from behind the red curtain.

MARIANNE. Did you just hear something?

The OTHERS, preoccupied, don't respond.

CLAUDIA. *Philippe!?* Attencion!

LEO. Screw it. Just pick a table, any table.

A TABLE HAS APPEARED, beautifully set with flowers and menus.

PAUL. This one looks good.

THEY seat themselves and take menus.

LEO. So this is, what, German Expressionist cuisine?

CLAUDIA. French Deconstructivist. That means nothing is what it seems. Philippe will prepare a steak so it tastes like, I dunno, flounder.

LEO. What if you want steak?

CLAUDIA. Order the tuna.

PAUL. If you want the chicken, order bean dip.

FRITZ (*pointedly, to* LEO). And if you want *pumpkin*...

PAUL (*freaking out at the word*). Pumpkin?

MARIANNE. Do they have pumpkin?

FRITZ (*smirking, to* RAFFAEL)....order *semolina*.

PAUL (*aside to* LEO). (She's penetrated the goddamn code!)

Another CHORD and ANOTHER SOB from behind the curtain, a little longer and a little louder, becoming a WAIL.

MARIANNE. I swear I hear someone crying.

LEO. Why would somebody cry in a restaurant?

MARIANNE. I've cried in many restaurants.

CHORD.

CLAUDIA. Garçonnn? Anybody...?

LEO *taps his glass. CHORD.*

LEO (*sings, mock French*).
    Mesdames, Monsieurs,
    Avant le mange,
    (*Raises his glass.*)
    To crème brûlée –

MARIANNE.
    To duck à l'orange –

PAUL (*raises his glass*).
    To sole meunière –

RAFFAEL (*raises his glass*).
    To Camembert –

CLAUDIA (*raises her glass*).
    To –

The WAIL stops momentarily as a FRENCH WAITRESS ENTERS, weeping quietly.

ACT ONE: THE ROAD   31

FRENCH WAITRESS. Bonjour. Bienvenue to Bistro À La Mode.

CLAUDIA. Hi there. Claudia Bursik-Zimmer. My husband and I are regulars here. Well, we've *eaten* here. Anyway, we wanted some brunch.

FRENCH WAITRESS. Brunch is past.

CLAUDIA. Okay, some lunch then.

FRENCH WAITRESS. Lunch is past.

CLAUDIA. What about – ?

FRENCH WAITRESS. Past, past, past!

MARIANNE. I hate to ask, but could we have some water?

FRENCH WAITRESS. Watteur? You want *watteur*?

THE FRENCH WAITRESS breaks down and sobs with hanging head.

CLAUDIA. What is it about water today?

FRENCH WAITRESS (*pulling herself together*). *Bon!* Do we 'ave questions – about le menu?

ANOTHER WAIL, and SOBBING, from behind the curtain.

LEO. Yeah, lemme get this straight. Nothing in here is what it seems?

FRENCH WAITRESS (*emotionally*). Non, non, non! That is passé! Our new menu is post-deconstructif. Everything now – (*Suppressing sobs.*) – is what it is!

SHE whips out a handkerchief with which, during the following, SHE dabs her eyes and occasionally her nose. SHE also resumes SOBBING and continues to do so throughout the following song, though the SOBS come in different flavors: whimpers, sniffles, lip-biting, etc.

(*Sings.*)
    We 'ave boeuf – (*Sob.*)
    That is actual boeuf – (*Suppresses a sob.*)
    On the actual hoeuf. (*Sobs.*)

We 'ave pigeon that's made out of pigeon, (*Sobs.*)
And a green salad (*Repressing sobs.*)
Made of just – (*Bites her lip.*)
Greens.

ANOTHER WAIL from behind the curtain, increasing, which this time CONTINUES under the following:

CLAUDIA. How is the pigeon prepared?

FRENCH WAITRESS (*hysterical*).
Does it matteur?
What does anything matteur?
(*Wearily.*) It is what it is.
Things are what they are.
La vie est la vie.

The GROUP looks up at her quizzically. SHE bites her lip to hold back tears for a moment, as MUSIC and WAILING continue underneath.

LEO. Okay. Everybody know what they want?

Before they can order, the FRENCH WAITRESS resumes singing.

FRENCH WAITRESS (*with heavy irony, à la Edith Piaf*).
Do we know what we want?
Does anyone know what they want?
As soon as we know what we want
And find what we want,
Life, she spits in our face.

The FRENCH WAITRESS literally spits.

PAUL. Any specials?

During the following, A SOMBER MAN crosses through from the direction of the kitchen, carrying CHURCH CANDLES, and EXITS with them behind the red curtain.

FRENCH WAITRESS (*checks her pad*).
Black-bean soup…
Blackened catfish…
Blackbird pudding…
Boudin noir…

> Black Sea blackberries
> In a chocolate gateau.
>
> (*Speaks.*) *Dark* chocolate. Dark dark dark…

LEO. Chicken Basquaise, baby. That's what I want.

The FRENCH WAITRESS *suddenly explodes into full torch song mode, during which the* OTHERS *study their menus, occasionally looking up at her briefly to listen.*

FRENCH WAITRESS.
> Sometimes you want too much,
> Too soon –
> And then it's too late.
> But what can you do
> If that's on your plate?
> (*Shrugs in resignation.*)
> You do what you can.

MUSIC and WAILING CONTINUE UNDER as ANOTHER WAITER *comes from the direction of the kitchen, carrying a wreath of flowers, and exits behind the red curtain.*

MARIANNE. What's going on back there?

FRENCH WAITRESS. Nothing. Nothing. C'est rien là.

MARIANNE. Is that a private room?

FRENCH WAITRESS. It is nothing. Really –

MARIANNE. But I adore private rooms!

MARIANNE *draws the curtain aside to reveal a BODY laid out on a table in a dark suit and a chef's toque, surrounded by MOURNERS singing a 'Dies Irae'.*

CLAUDIA. Oh. My. God.

PAUL. Philippe…!

MUSIC and MOURNERS CONTINUE underneath.

LEO. That's Philippe?

FRENCH WAITRESS. That *was* Philippe.

LEO. He's just kidding, right?

FRENCH WAITRESS. Monsieur, he was French. He 'ave no sense of humeur.

(*Sings.*)
'E was what 'e was.
We are what we are.
(*Shrugging.*) It is what it is…

(*Spoken.*) So. Are we ready to ordeur?

MUSIC ENDS. The FRENCH WAITRESS *takes out a pencil.* FRENCH WAITRESS *exits.*

PAUL. *Can we get OUT of here, please?*

CLAUDIA. *Get a Health inspection*, for Christ's sake!

MARIANNE. My *word*! And in the party room?!

RAFFAEL. There is the Osteria Zeno. Very close by.

LEO. The closer the better. Back to square one. Everybody into the car!

The SCENE CHANGES.

Road 3

THEY resume walking down the country road but, as they do, everything suddenly stutters and lurches a bit. The GROUP stumbles with bemusement rather than alarm, then regains its balance and smoothly resumes its 'ride'.

MARIANNE. Such an afternoon!

CLAUDIA. Afternoon? It's almost suppertime!

LEO. Like they say: *Later than we think*.

PAUL. Yeah.

MARIANNE. I adore afternoons. They're my favorite.

FRITZ. What?

MARIANNE. What?

FRITZ. Favorite what?

MARIANNE. Favorite time of the day, darling.

CLAUDIA (*to* FRITZ). Leave it alone.

SINISTER ANOMALIES begin to show up on the horizon: a discolored cloud, a tilted house, a suspended animal. Only PAUL *takes note.*

PAUL (*looking around, uneasily*). Something's happening, Something very odd.

A brief outburst of CACOPHONY in the ORCHESTRA. No one takes notice except PAUL, *who senses it. Then the blithe VAMP resumes.*

LEO. Odder than the food situation in this town?

FRITZ (*to* RAFFAEL, PAUL *and* LEO). Okay, boys. Shall we talk semolina?

PAUL (*playing innocent*). 'Semolina'?

FRITZ. *Drug money.*

PAUL. Oh, that semolina…

FRITZ. Fifty million bucks or I tell the Feds about your pumpkin cartel.

LEO. What're you planning to do with fifty mil?

FRITZ. Destroy capitalism.

A small pause. LEO *and* RAFFAEL *explode into laughter.*

PAUL. Do we have that much in the, you know, the silo?

FRITZ. You want to save your asses, fifty mil's the price.

LEO. You can't dig into your trust fund for that? (*Off* FRITZ's *look.*) Oh, I'm sorry. Did I say a dirty word?

FRITZ. Okay. I'm calling.

RAFFAEL. Gentlemen? Do we save ourselves and 'destroy capitalism'?

LEO. Sounds like a bargain to me. Paul?

PAUL *shrugs 'yes', still feeling uneasy.*

Raffi?

RAFFAEL *gives a vigorous thumbs-up.*

It's a deal! You got robbed, kid.

MARIANNE / CLAUDIA (*sings*).
>What a perfect,
>What a perfect day!

PAUL.
>Something's happening,

MARIANNE / CLAUDIA.
>On a day like today,
>What could ever go wrong?

PAUL.
>Can't you feel it? I can feel it…
>Something's going on…

MARIANNE. I know! It's like me blanking on this thing I was supposed to do.

PAUL.
>Something doesn't fit,
>And I don't like it, not one bit.

CLAUDIA. You know what's wrong, Mare? Your brain is *on the fritz*!

CLAUDIA *and* MARIANNE *howl at that.*

RAFFAEL. Ah, the sight of beautiful ladies laughing. And behold! Osteria Zeno!

LEO. Everybody out of the car!

THE SCENE CHANGES to…

Scene Four: Osteria Zeno

THEY ENTER the restaurant. A TABLE APPEARS.

MARIANNE. Why, this place –

FRITZ *picks up with her.*

MARIANNE / FRITZ.... is perfectly *adorable*!

PAUL. Check this out, guys. Antipasto, a bottle of good Chianti. Food at last!

ITALIAN WAITER *ENTERS.*

ITALIAN WAITER. Buona sera! Benvenuti tutti all' Osteria Zeno!

RAFFAEL. Ciao, raggazzo!

ITALIAN WAITER (*'Huh?'*). Che...?

CLAUDIA. Listen. You not having a funeral today, are you?

ITALIAN WAITER. A *funeral*, Signora...? *Today?*

CLAUDIA. Never mind, just gimme a menu.

ITALIAN WAITER. Prego, prego.

THEY seat themselves.

MARIANNE. How is the food here?

ITALIAN WAITER (*passing out menus*). Divino, signora. I eat her myself. Acqua? Acqua?

MARIANNE. Yes, pl–

LEO. *NO.* Let's just order.

ITALIAN WAITER. So no acqua?

MARIANNE *is raising her hand quietly.*

LEO. *NO ACQUA.*

CHORD.

(*Sings.*)
Ladies and gents,
Before we dine,
Let us thank the Lord
For cheese and wine,

MARIANNE.
For eggs and cream,

CLAUDIA.
For bread and meat,

PAUL.
　For –

LEO. Yeah yeah yeah. Good enough. Let's eat! Before something bad happens.

HE is interrupted as COLONEL MARTIN *ENTERS, blowing A WHISTLE.*

BINGO!

COL. MARTIN. This restaurant is closed by order of the U.S. Army!

ITALIAN WAITER (*grabbing the menus and exiting*). Goodbye! We close now! Addio! Ciao!

COL. MARTIN (*showing his badge*). Colonel Jock Martin, Homeland Security.

MARIANNE. But, Colonel, we're starving!

COL. MARTIN. Madam, have you ever seen a person starve to death? They tell me it's not a pretty sight.

CLAUDIA. What is all this, anyway?

COL. MARTIN. My unit's on the lookout for an international drug cartel.

PAUL. A drug cartel? Really? Around here?

COL. MARTIN. We know the leaders are somewhere in this restaurant right now.

FRITZ (*indicates* RAFFAEL, LEO *and* PAUL). These men run a drug cartel.

MARIANNE. Oh, shush. (*Excusing* FRITZ *to the* COLONEL.) My sister the socialist.

COL. MARTIN. Apparently the operation's run through some Mediterranean rat-hole called Moranda.

FRITZ. This is the Morandan ambassador.

COL. MARTIN. I'm honored, sir.

FRITZ. Colonel, these men are the people you're…!

ACT ONE: THE ROAD 39

FRITZ stops abruptly as a SOLDIER ENTERS and salutes.

SOLDIER. The place is surrounded, sir. Should we move in?

A brief outburst of CACOPHONY in the ORCHESTRA, like the one PAUL heard on the road. FRITZ is the only one who hears it.

FRITZ (*seeing the SOLDIER, bursts into SONG*).
    Oh, my God – !

The OTHERS look at her, startled, then follow her gaze.

    That soldier – !

COL. MARTIN (*correcting her, sings*).
    That lieutenant –

FRITZ.
    – That lieutenant
    Is so –
    (*Searches for the word.*)

MARIANNE.
    Soulful.

CLAUDIA.
    Gorgeous!

RAFFAEL.
    Dreamy!

COL. MARTIN.
    Funny you say dreamy. You see –
    My soulful gorgeous lieutenant
    Had a fascinating dream last night.

MUSIC STOPS. EVERYONE looks at each other and rises to leave.

No, really, it's a good one.

EVERYONE sits.

At ease, Lieutenant! Tell us your dream.

Dreamlike MUSIC begins, as THE GROUP starts to nibble hors d'oeuvres and sip wine.

SOLDIER.
> I was in a café
> Which looked somewhat like this,
> Sitting next to a girl
> (*To* FRITZ.) Who looked something like you.
> And she whispered her name.
> I've forgotten her name,
> But the name was like music –

FRITZ.
> 'Fritz.'

SOLDIER.
> That was it!
> That was it!
> (*To the OTHERS.*)
> And you and you were there,
> And you and you and you –
> All wearing shrouds.

The ITALIAN WAITER *ENTERS and offers SHROUDS.*

ITALIAN WAITER. A shroud, anyone? A shroud?

SOLDIER.
> And then I noticed that you'd all been dead for years.

ITALIAN WAITER. A shroud, Signora?

CLAUDIA.
> SHHHH!

ITALIAN WAITER *EXITS.*

SOLDIER.
> Except for the girl with a name like a rainbow…

FRITZ.
> 'Fritz.'

SOLDIER (*looking at* FRITZ, *thunderstruck*).
> Oh, my God – !

FRITZ (*looking at the* SOLDIER, *thunderstruck*).
> Oh, my God – !

THEY gaze at each other in paralyzed silence as the ORCHESTRA plays a thunderous and rapturous PIANO

CONCERTO for longer than necessary. COLONEL
MARTIN *and the OTHERS exchange impatient glances, as
the MUSIC CONTINUES underneath. Finally,* LEO *speaks,
in rhythm.*

LEO. That was it? That's the dream?

SOLDIER (*recovering his composure, sings*).
    Then my mother came in –

PAUL (*knowingly*). Of course.

SOLDIER.
    She was holding a sheep.

    SOLDIER'S MOTHER *ENTERS pulling a STUFFED
    SHEEP.*

PAUL (*shrugs*). What else.

SOLDIER.
    And she said to me:

SOLDIER'S MOTHER (*as* SOLDIER *mouths the words*).
    Honey, stop dreaming!

    MOTHER *and SHEEP EXIT.*

SOLDIER.
    So I started to wake,
    But the girl with the name
    Took a hold of my hand and said –

FRITZ (*as* SOLDIER *mouths the words*).
    'Never forget me.'

SOLDIER.
    Though how could I forget her
    When we never had met?
    Then I looked in her eyes,
    And I thought:
    Oh, my God – !

FRITZ.
    Oh, my God – !

The rapturous CONCERTO plays again, as the SOLDIER
and FRITZ *gaze into each other's eyes.*

SOLDIER.
> – It's the end of the world.
> There is nothing but you.
> I've been looking for love all my life.
> I've no farther to go.
> I want only to be with you,
> Live with you,
> Die with you.
> That much I know.
> Then my mother came in.

MOTHER *re-enters, with SHEEP.*

PAUL. Again?

SOLDIER (*looking around the room*).
> And I saw that the sheep was stuffed
> And the sky was cloth
> And the clouds were just paint
> And the food was just rubber…

MUSIC CONTINUES UNDER.

CLAUDIA (*spits out an olive*). He's right! It is rubber!

LEO (*spitting out the wine*). This isn't wine, it's goddamn cherry soda!

RAFFAEL. It's too bad. I was rather enjoying the Brie.

SOLDIER (*sings*).
> Then a curtain went up –

LIGHT CHANGE here.

> And I realized we were all in a play.
> On a stage.
> In a theater.

THEY ALL look out into the audience.

MARIANNE (*peering*). Who are those people…?

LEO. What the *fuck*?!

PAUL. *I don't know my lines!*

ACT ONE: THE ROAD   43

LIGHTS CHANGE BACK and THEY return their attention to the SOLDIER, *except for* MARIANNE, *who keeps glancing nervously at the* AUDIENCE.

SOLDIER.
> Then I looked in her eyes,
> And I thought:

The CONCERTO again.

> If it's only a play –

FRITZ.
> Omigod.
> Omigod, omigod –!

SOLDIER.
> – Still, it's given me you.

FRITZ.
> Omigod – !

The following lyrics overlap.

SOLDIER.
> I've been looking so long…

FRITZ.
> This is not what I need –

SOLDIER.
> You are all that I need –

FRITZ.
> Not yet –

SOLDIER.
> In my life –

FRITZ.
> Not now.

SOLDIER.
> Only you –

FRITZ.
> I don't have any room in my life –

SOLDIER.
> – And me –

FRITZ.
> For this –

SOLDIER.
> For now –

FRITZ.
> For you –

SOLDIER.
> Forever!
> All I need is to be with you
> Live with you,
> Die with you.
> That much I know.

FRITZ.
> I've got too much to do,
> There's just not enough time –
> Then I look in your eyes
> And I think, 'Holy crap,
> It's the end of the – '

SOLDIER.
> Then a train passed through…

LOUD WHISTLES as A TRAIN ROARS through the restaurant. CACOPHONY in the ORCHESTRA, which gradually SUBSIDES as the TRAIN exits.

MUSIC CONTINUES.

> And I suddenly knew
> It was not just the end of the world,
> But the end of the play.

> (*Offhand, speaks.*) And the end of my dream.

A moment's SILENCE.

FRITZ (*softly, sings into the silence*).
> Omigod…
> Omigod…

MUSIC resumes briefly, then DIES AWAY.

MARIANNE. Well, you are really smitten, darling.

RAFFAEL. I thought you were a gay.

FRITZ. I'm exploring! All right?

LEO. Oh, no. OH, NO! FRITZ IS CHANGING! (*Fake heart attack.*) GAAAAAAAAAAH!

MARIANNE. Leo.

LEO. GAAAAAAAAAAAAHHHHHHH!

PAUL. Hey, we've had enough corpses for one day.

COL. MARTIN. Funny you should mention corpses. You see, my parents were brutally murdered for twenty-six dollars and fifteen cents when I was a child –

PAUL (*putting him off*). Yeah, yeah, great, thanks –

LEO. No, I want to hear. Murdered for twenty-six dollars, huh?

COL. MARTIN. And fifteen cents.

LEO. It wasn't with something like a… thirty-eight-caliber Smith & Wesson?

COL. MARTIN. It was a thirty-eight-caliber Smith & Wesson.

LEO. Maybe someplace like… I don't know, Utica?

COL. MARTIN. Utica it was.

MARIANNE. Darling, you're from Utica.

CLAUDIA. MY SUGAR IS DROPPING!

RAFFAEL. My friends! Why don't we all go to the Embassy for dinner? I will call right now! Brunnhilde can start cooking!

MARIANNE / PAUL / CLAUDIA. Hooray!

RAFFAEL takes out his PHONE to make a call.

MARIANNE. Colonel Martin, you have to join us!

LEO. No, no, Marianne – you don't want to…

MARIANNE. We can discuss true crime! I love true crime! Will you come, Colonel? And your poetic lieutenant? Please?

COL. MARTIN. Actually, Ma'am, we haven't had a square meal all day.

PAUL. Well, neither have we!

LEO. So let's go find one!

THEY all make to leave. ITALIAN WAITER *ENTERS with a BILL.*

ITALIAN WAITER. Eh, scusi, scusi, signori! Il conto.

LEO. What is that…

ITALIAN WAITER. The *bill*. You pay the bill now.

LEO. A bill – for what? Rubber Brie? Cherry soda?

ITALIAN WAITER. Oh, you think all this comes for free, eh? No! You pay!

LEO (*glancing at the BILL*). Two hundred fif–? I'm not paying that! Screw you, paisano! And everybody else – into the car!

ITALIAN WAITER. You think this is the end? This is not the end! (*'Filth of a whore! You thief! You prick!':*) Sporco di puttana! Tu ladro! Tu strunz!

HE is still shouting 'LADRI! AIUTO! LADRI!' ('Thieves! Help! Thieves!') as THE SCENE CHANGES.

Road 4

THE GROUP, now with COLONEL MARTIN *and* SOLDIER, *resume their 'ride', walking down the country road. Evening's falling. The 'Road' vamp is heard.*

MARIANNE. Did you leave a tip?

LEO. Here's a tip: *don't serve fake food.*

(*Sings.*)
   If it isn't the food –

There's a slight stumble.

CLAUDIA.
　　If it isn't –

Another stumble.

MARIANNE.
　　It's always something.

FRITZ. Will we always be together? Forever?

SOLDIER. Forever is not long enough.

FRITZ (*sings*).
　　What a perfect day!

MARIANNE. Ah, young love. And it's springtime! Almost. Wait a minute, wait a minute! (*Grabs* LEO*'s arm.*) Leo. Oh, *Leo*!

LEO. Yes.

MARIANNE. Darling, I've got it! The thing I was supposed to do today!

The tiniest pause.

No I don't. I *had* it.

CLAUDIA. Almost.

LEO. Raffi, is this one hell of a creature here? Am I the luckiest bastard in the whole wide world?

RAFFAEL. What bastard would not be, with such a wife…

　　RAFFAEL *sidles up to* MARIANNE. *TANGO music starts.*

(*Quietly.*) I have to have you.

MARIANNE (*brightly, to the GROUP, putting him off*). You know where I like spring the best? Versailles.

Holds up her hand.

I know, April, yes, in Paris, but Versailles –

The DIALOGUE becomes RHYTHMIC.

RAFFAEL (*whispering into her ear*). God, you are so hot.

MARIANNE (*sotto voce*). Raffi, really –

RAFFAEL (*sings, softly but ardently*).
> Marianne,
> Don't you know that you
> Are Versailles
> (*Intimately.*) To me?

MARIANNE. Raffi – !

RAFFAEL.
> Marianne,
> My municipal rose.

MARIANNE. Municipal?

RAFFAEL (*flustered, correcting himself*). Munificent... Magnificent...

> (*Sings, his ardor increasing.*) Marianne,
> I've known women before you,
> But the way I adore you –

MARIANNE (*glancing at* LEO). Please, this is very inconvenient.

RAFFAEL (*insinuatingly*).
> Do I bore you?

MARIANNE. Well...

RAFFAEL. I was joking.

MARIANNE. Oh.

RAFFAEL.
> Marianne,
> Don't you know this is do or die
> To me?
> Marianne,
> My inedible rose...

MARIANNE. Inedible?

RAFFAEL (*correcting himself furiously*). Incredible! Incredible!

> (*Sings.*) Marianne,
> Won't you give me a chance?

I can tell at a glance
You are everything France –

(*Murmurs into her ear.*) God, you are so hot –

MARIANNE (*flinching*). Raffi – !

RAFFAEL (*to* MARIANNE). I mean French. (*Low and sultry.*) (I have to have you.)

MARIANNE (*tempted, wilting*). (Do you really, Raffi…?)

LEO. So, Raffi…

RAFFAEL. Later, Leo. I'm seducing your wife.

(*Sings.*)
Marianne…

(*Spoken.*) Oh, look, here's the Embassy!

The SCENE CHANGES to…

Scene Five: The Morandan Embassy

RAFFAEL *leads them into the Embassy. They're in awe.*

RAFFAEL (*calls*). Windsor!

MARIANNE. Isn't it sublime?

LEO. Raffi, you been holding out on us! This is magnificent!

MARIANNE. And will you look at that ceiling?! That is classic rococo! Or is it baroque? I can never tell the difference. I always say 'barococo'. The clients never seem to notice.

CLAUDIA. I always love being here. Six bedrooms, ten servants to wait on you?

PAUL. When were you ever here…?

CLAUDIA. Oh, I don't – I never – I just mean, you know, *wow*. Right?

RAFFAEL. WINDSOR!? – That's odd… WINDSOR!

LEO. So what's this joint worth, Raffi? Thirty mil, forty mil?

MARIANNE. Money, money, money. You know what I love about all this? It's so aggressively *un*-middle class!

PAUL. Whatever middle class means these days.

CLAUDIA. Yeah. Everybody talks about 'the middle class'.

LEO. But nobody ever does anything about it.

THEY all howl at that.

MARIANNE. Fritzie does! You're overthrowing it, aren't you, darling?

LEO. Yeah, what happened to Armageddon, Fritz?

FRITZ. Armageddon… *Oh, my God.* The Revolution!

FRITZ reaches into her pocket for her PHONE, but the SOLDIER grabs her and draws her to him.

SOLDIER. This… is the Revolution. This moment.

FRITZ wriggles away, whips out her PHONE and frantically dials.

FRITZ. That's beautiful, but we're not going to be together forever unless I call off the end of the world.

SHE finishes dialing.

SOLDIER. You're amazing.

FRITZ (*to her phone*). 'Voicem…'?! No, I don't *want VOICEMAIL*!

SOLDIER. Kiss me, Fritz.

FRITZ. Yeah, but… Yeah, but… The end of the world…

FRITZ and the SOLDIER KISS. She thoughtlessly closes her phone.

CLAUDIA. Well I have to eat something or I'm going to go INSANE.

RAFFAEL. Where is he? WINDSOR!

WINDSOR *ENTERS, a perfect English butler.*

WINDSOR. Good evening, Your Excellency.

RAFFAEL. Windsor, where were you? All is well here?

WINDSOR. Tip-top, sir, very well indeed.

RAFFAEL. Supper is ready?

WINDSOR. Your call was rather short notice. Cook was thinking perhaps we could serve *you*, roasted on a spit with a candy apple in your mouth and plantains popping out of your arse.

Everyone stares in stupefaction.

A little joke, sir.

THEY laugh, relieved.

RAFFAEL. Ah, yes. English humor!

WINDSOR. Actually, Brunnhilde has made boeuf Bordelaise.

THEY ALL make ecstatic 'mmmms' and 'ohhhs' and 'yeses'.

(*To* MARIANNE.) May I take your peignoir, madam?

MARIANNE. He's funny. Leo, we should get one of these. [*i.e., a butler.*]

WINDSOR (*clapping his hands*). McGogg! The cocktails!

McGOGG *ENTERS, a strange, hunched maid shoving a drinks cart.*

CLAUDIA. Liquor at last!

McGOGG *slouches around the room handing out MARTINIS.*

WINDSOR (*holding out a GLASS for* CLAUDIA). I presume you all drink gin martinis?

CLAUDIA. I guess we do now!

SHE takes it and sips.

Oh my God, oh my God, you are a lifesaver, I could fuck you right here on the floor.

DOORBELL.

RAFFAEL. Windsor, is that the doorbell? At this hour…?

WINDSOR. I will check, sir.

WINDSOR *EXITS.*

COL. MARTIN. Funny thing, Your Excellency. The headquarters of that drug cartel have been traced to this very zipcode.

RAFFAEL. Oh, 'cartel, cartel'. Co-lo-nel, you seem to be obsessed!

WINDSOR *ENTERS.*

WINDSOR. Excuse me, sir. There's a gentleman here to see you.

RAFFAEL. A gentleman? What kind of gentleman…?

A BISHOP *ENTERS: white chasuble, mitre and crozier.*

BISHOP. Peace be unto this house. Peace be unto all of you, my brothers and sisters. Peace and harmony and abundance –

RAFFAEL. I am very sorry – Bishop, is it? We were just headed to dinner.

BISHOP (*making to leave*). Okay.

MARIANNE. No, no, wait, I've never met a bishop! – But aren't you supposed to be clad in radiant scarlet?

BISHOP. Scarlet is higher. I love your slippers, by the way. Very fetching.

LEO. Maybe another time, Your Holiness – ?

BISHOP. This won't take a second. (*To* McGOGG, *bringing him a drink.*) Pre-poured martinis. Wonderful! Please, stay near, my child. This may relate to you.

BISHOP *sips a bit off the martini. MUSIC.*

(*Speaks in rhythm.*)
  Now, does anybody here have any spiritual needs…?
  Spiritual needs…?
  Anyone…?

LEO (*politely*). No.

He glances impatiently at MARIANNE.

BISHOP.
>Well, do any of you think about the meaning of life?
>Meaning of life…?
>Any of you…?

McGOGG *raises her hand. A tinkling SOUND.*

>Good. Anybody else?

MUSIC stops, one CHORD holding and FADING UNDERNEATH.

>Meaning of Life? God? Death? Anyone for purgatory?

Nobody bites.

>(*Noting* CLAUDIA*'s footwear.*) Now *those* shoes are cute… Are they Fendi?

RAFFAEL. Bishop – please – how can we help you? Practically.

MUSIC resumes.

BISHOP (*sings*).
>Well, I could use a job,
>You could give me a job.
>I'm a terrible priest.

As THEY look at him, surprised:

>No, I'm in the wrong job.
>I keep spilling the wine,
>I keep crumbling the wafers,
>I have no charisma.

Awkward PAUSE, as no one argues the point.

>In the middle of Mass,
>All I think is:
>My miter
>Should be tighter.
>I mean, why a bishop?
>Why not an anarchist?

>   Why not a bartender?
>   I could be anything!
>   Why a bishop?!
>
>   Don't get me wrong,
>   I love the church,
>   And I don't only mean the clothes,
>   I mean the statues and the windows
>   And the rows of yearning people
>   And the special parking
>   And oh, the music – !
>   What else to call it but 'divine'?
>   And then of course, there's God.

HE PAUSES briefly again.

>   Don't get me wrong,
>   I love my God,
>   Though I don't always understand Him
>   Or agree.
>
>   Like, do we really need the droughts
>   And the floods
>   And the plagues
>   (*His voice rising.*)
>   And the earthquakes
>   And the universal suffering and –

HE notices EVERYONE staring at him.

>   See?
>   Does that sound like a priest?

(MARIANNE*'s shoes again.*) *Really* fetching.

(*Sings.*)
>   Now if I were a cook,
>   (I'm not bad as a cook)
>   I could work as a cook
>   In a nice country house…

MARIANNE. Darling?

BISHOP.
>   …with a fabulous terrace…

ACT ONE: THE ROAD 55

LEO (*speaks in rhythm, curt but polite*). We have a cook.

BISHOP (*critically*).
>Where they could use a gardener…

MARIANNE. You're a gardener, too?

BISHOP.
>I could learn.

LEO. No.

BISHOP.
>Wouldn't anybody like to have their windows washed?

LEO. *No*.

BISHOP.
>Their sinks repaired?

CLAUDIA. No.

BISHOP.
>Their faith restored?

RAFFAEL. No.

BISHOP.
>Their lives renewed?

PAUL. No.

BISHOP.
>Their anything anything?

ALL FOUR. NO!

BISHOP.
>All I want is a job,
>Where I'd be of some use,
>Where I'd know who I was,
>Where I'd make people feel that they matter,
>Although none of us does –

(*Hastily, reverting to speech.*) In the big picture, I mean…

(*Sings.*)
>Something different, at least.
>God knows,

I'm a terrible priest.
And if anyone should know,
God knows, it's God.

MUSIC ENDS.

MARIANNE. Oh, Leo, can't we help him? He needs some meaning in his life!

COL. MARTIN. Don't we all. (*To* BISHOP.) You see, my parents were brutally murdered back in Utica –

LEO (*cutting him off*). Listen, listen, why don't we discuss this over food. We have room, don't we, Raffi?

RAFFAEL. By all means.

BISHOP. I am rather peckish.

RAFFAEL. Windsor, another chair.

MARIANNE. Hurray! You can sit next to me.

LEO. Good. Well, here's to a happy, pre-poured evening!

A LOUD GUNSHOT.

EVERYONE hears it and goes perfectly still.

BISHOP. *JESUS!*

FRITZ. No, no, no…

PAUL. What was that?

LEO. Maybe another waiter.

FRITZ. That was the sound of the Revolution.

FRITZ *takes out her PHONE and starts pounding it frantically.*

CLAUDIA. That was the sound of *the city*.

(*Sings.*)
If it's not some alarm,
It's a backfire.

LEO.
Either that or the blat
Of a horn

RAFFAEL.
>It's but one of the joys
>Of the city: the noise –

WINDSOR.
>Sir, as sure as the day I was born
>That was a shot.

Simultaneous:

MARIANNE. How exciting! Let's go see!
PAUL. Maybe it was a gunshot…
CLAUDIA. A gunshot in *this* neighborhood?
FRITZ. Listen! The Revolution is starting!
RAFFAEL. Absolutely absurd!
LEO. It's the city, what's the big deal?
SOLDIER. But Fritz, who cares what it was!
COL. MARTIN. I think I know what a gunshot sounds like.
BISHOP. My Lord, how terrible – !

PAUL. I told you –

>(*Sings.*)
>>Something's happening,
>>Something's going on…

FRITZ (*muttering urgently into her phone*). Come on, Inferno. Come on!

MARIANNE. O, it's not the end of the world, Fritzie!

FRITZ. This time it is!

A LOUD GONG is heard.

WINDSOR. Dinner is served!

The FEAST awaiting them is revealed.

CLAUDIA (*screams*). *AAAAAAHHHHHHHHHHHHHH!* FOOD!

LEO (*sings, faster than before*).
>Ladies and gents,
>Let's do it fast.
>We thank you, Lord,
>For food at last –

THEY ALL raise their glasses, except FRITZ.

PAUL.
>And just to make the day complete:
>(*Gestures to* RAFFAEL.)
>To you –

BISHOP.
>To you –

CLAUDIA.
>To you –

MARIANNE.
>To you –

LEO.
>To you –

RAFFAEL.
>To you –

COL. MARTIN.
>To you –

SOLDIER.
>To you –

WE HEAR A CELLPHONE RING. WINDSOR *takes out his phone.*

WINDSOR (*into his phone, quietly*). Inferno here.

FRITZ sees WINDSOR *on his phone and realizes she's talking to him.*

FRITZ. You...?

WINDSOR (*into his phone*). Bon appetit, Apocalypse. Do enjoy your evening.

WINDSOR *hangs up.* FRITZ *stands, shocked.*

LEO. Let's eat!

MARIANNE sees that FRITZ is by herself and takes her arm. LEO takes her other arm to lead her into dinner.

POLICE SIRENS and MORE GUNSHOTS are heard in the distance as…

ALL (*EXCEPT* FRITZ, *sing*).
　What a perfect day!

THEY all head in to dinner.

END OF ACT ONE.

ACT TWO: THE ROOM

Scene One: The Embassy Salon, After Dinner

Old-world elegance. The room's only entrance is a high, wide portal. There's a door to a closet. A sofa and chairs. A grandfather clock. A large bouquet in a vase. An antique Chinese jar. Shelves of fine books. A baby-grand piano. A tapestry that somehow recalls the field and road of Act One.

LEO *digests uncomfortably on the sofa.* MARIANNE, *tipsy, primps at a mirror.* RAFFAEL *hovers nearby.* PAUL *sits at his wife's feet as* CLAUDIA *works her phone. The* SOLDIER *regards* FRITZ *as SHE paces the room nervously.* McGOGG *slouches about, gathering dirty cups.* WINDSOR *tours the room with the drinks cart.* COLONEL MARTIN, *investigating the room, looks into the closet.*

We hear the VAMP that opened Act One, briefly. The BISHOP, *at the piano, noodles along.*

LEO *BURPS loudly.*

MARIANNE. Do I hear music?

LEO (*groaning*). Must've eaten something...

CLAUDIA. I wonder what the kids are up to.

PAUL. You calling them?

CLAUDIA. No, just surfing.

    FRITZ *pulls* WINDSOR *aside for a private talk.*

FRITZ. (Hey. Hey, you. What's going on out there?)

WINDSOR. (Patience, Apocalypse. All will be revealed.)

MARIANNE. Is my hair a horror?

    LEO *BURPS loudly.*

    The VAMP continues.

RAFFAEL. Not at all, it's beautiful.

MARIANNE. Oh, stop.

COL. MARTIN. What you're playing, that is beautiful.

BISHOP. Really…?

FRITZ (*stops pacing a moment; an outburst*). Christ…!

FRITZ resumes pacing.

The TANGO from the opening of Part One replaces the VAMP.

RAFFAEL (*sotto voce, to* MARIANNE).
I have to have you.
Now, more than ever.

LEO *BURPS.*

WINDSOR *moves the cart to* LEO.

WINDSOR (*to* LEO). A digestif –

Slightly ominous pause.

Sir?

LEO. No, thanks.

FRITZ (*calls to* WINDSOR). Over here, pal.

The SOLDIER *puts his hand on her arm to stop her from having another drink.* FRITZ *shakes him free and takes the drink.*

PAUL (*sings*).
I have to say
I didn't think
The carrots had much lilt.

MUSIC STOPS momentarily.

CLAUDIA. Oh, you always say that.

A delicate PERCUSSIVE SOUND. CLAUDIA *and* PAUL *exchange air-kisses.*

MARIANNE. Isn't it wonderful to be doing something different for a change?

MUSIC RESUMES. Everything exactly as before:

RAFFAEL (*sotto voce, to* MARIANNE).
>I have to have you.
>Now, more than ever.

LEO *BURPS.*

WINDSOR *wheels the cart back to* LEO.

WINDSOR (*to* LEO). A digestif –

Slightly ominous pause.

Sir?

LEO. No, thanks.

FRITZ (*calls to* WINDSOR). Over here, pal.

The SOLDIER *puts his hand on her arm to stop her from having another drink.* FRITZ *shakes him free and takes the drink.*

PAUL (*sings*).
>I have to say
>I didn't think
>The carrots had much lilt.

MUSIC STOPS momentarily.

CLAUDIA. Oh, you always say that.

A delicate PERCUSSIVE SOUND. CLAUDIA *and* PAUL *air-kiss.*

MARIANNE. Isn't it wonderful to be doing something different for a change?

MUSIC RESUMES.

LEO. You know, I've eaten a carrot every – (*Burps.*) day for forty – (*Burps.*) years – (*Holds his stomach.*) Jeez, what is this?

PAUL (*sings*).
>I have nothing but praise
>For the beef Bordelaise,
>But she fucked up the glaze
>On the peas.

ACT TWO: THE ROOM 63

MARIANNE. Oh, please. Peas, peas, peas, who cares? Here we are in Eden!

CLAUDIA. And then some.

RAFFAEL. I love this expression. 'And then some.' Did you have fun? *And then some!* Was it good? *And then some!* People tell me less is more and I say, no! *More* is more*! AND THEN SOME!*

The BISHOP, *at the piano, accompanies* MARIANNE.

MARIANNE (*sings*).
 Are we not blessed?

PAUL (*to* LEO, *pointing to his stomach*). Oversalted. That's the problem.

MARIANNE.
 We should all feel blessed.

Spreads her arms.

LEO, CLAUDIA. All I feel is bloated.

THEY chuckle at each other and touch their fingers to the tips of their noses in camaraderie.

MARIANNE.
 Blessed with this –
 (*Gestures to the room.*)
 Blessed with these –
 (*Gestures to the objects in the room.*)
 Blessed with carpets, cushions, flowers –
 All this beauty that is ours,
 All these books!
 All these polished leather books!

As LEO *gives the others a 'Get her!' look.*

 I don't mean to read –
 No, no, not to read,
 No, I mean the way it looks!

FRITZ. Not that we want to be superficial.

MARIANNE (*blithely defiant*).

I like things to shine –
Shoot me.
I like things to glow.

Why can't I be free
To like what I see
And not what I know?

Raises her glass in a toast, takes a drink.

(*Looking around.*)
I'd like to live life, all my life,
In this room,
In this gorgeous goddamn room –
I don't mean in this room,
But I mean in this room,
With these textures and these surfaces,
All these touchy-feely surfaces –
(*Archly.*) Goodness me, how superficial,

Swigs what remains of her drink.

Well, what's wrong with superficial?
I want things to shine –
(*To* WINDSOR, *waving her glass.*) Hit me.
(*Back to the others.*)
Is that so bizarre?
I want things to gleam.
To be what they seem,
And not what they are.
(*As* WINDSOR *fills her glass.*) Call me…

LEO. Bourgeoir?

MARIANNE. Bourgeois, for God's sake.

Shrugs to the others.

I don't need to read between the lines,
The lines are just fine –
As long as they shine.
(*Takes a drink; exuberantly.*) Give me what shines!
Give me –

LEO. Hold it! (*BURPS.*)

MARIANNE.
 …this.

RAFFAEL. Well, mimis amichichis, it has been a lovely day – and evening – but now I must wish you all a fond goodnight. Windsor, the door, please. And for now – adidio!

WINDSOR stands at the portal to guide them out as all RISE except the BISHOP, still improvising at the piano. The following DIALOGUE and ACTION are in RHYTHM.

PAUL. It was lovely, Raffi.

CLAUDIA. Perfect! And who cares about the meal, anyway?

SHE air-kisses him on each cheek.

RAFFAEL (*quietly, to* CLAUDIA). (Until Tuesday at two!) – Your Holiness?

BISHOP (*rising from the piano*). A truly joyful evening. God bless you, sir.

MARIANNE. Time, Leo.

LEO (*reluctantly rising*). Yeah, yeah. Back to square one.

MARIANNE. O, must he say that all the time?

COL. MARTIN. Back to barracks, Lieutenant.

SOLDIER. Fritz? One final look at the stars?

FRITZ. If they're still there.

A general simultaneous CACOPHONY of goodbyes:

PAUL. Thanks, Raffi!
LEO. It was great!
CLAUDIA. Love you, sweetie!
MARIANNE. À tout à l'heure!
COLONEL. An honor, sir!
BISHOP. Wonderful!

The GUESTS have reached the portal of the room, to exit. SUDDENLY:

MUSIC: the VAMP from the opening of the show.

THEY STOP as one, shy of the portal, hesitant. A CHORD holds underneath. After a BEAT, the following lines are SUNG and/or SPOKEN IN RHYTHM, some overlapping. When they are SPOKEN, they are accompanied by melodies on solo instruments in the orchestra, making the sequence a sort of murmured mini-chorale.

MARIANNE (*to the group, sings*).
    Such a gorgeous room…

A BRIEF MOMENT of SILENCE. THEY PAUSE and look at each other, as if not certain what to do next.

CLAUDIA (*to* RAFFAEL).
    Maybe just one more drink…

LEO (*nods to* MARIANNE, *glancing at his watch*).
    It's not really that late…

RAFFAEL. No, no, really! I must insist. Into the night with you, per favavere! And for now, adidio!

Again THEY start to exit, except for LEO, *who slumps back in his chair, loosening his tie. Again the VAMP, and again THEY hesitate at the portal, SINGING and SPEAKING in RHYTHM, overlapping.*

MARIANNE.
    Will you look at these books?…

PAUL.
    It's the shank of the evening…

CLAUDIA.
    I've got nothing to do in the morning…

LEO.
    One more burp…

FRITZ (*belligerently*).
    What's the rush, Raffi?

COL. MARTIN.
    Maybe just one more brandy…

CLAUDIA.
    … not till nine o'clock anyway…

PAUL.
>Hey! Why don't we just spend the night?

LEO.
>That's a fantastic idea!

CLAUDIA.
>Absolutely.

RAFFAEL.
>You're joking.

CLAUDIA. We can stay right in here!

MARIANNE. It'll be an adventure!   LEO. We can stay right in here!

MARIANNE.
>And I'm already in my nightie!

LEO. We can stay right in here! We can stay right down here!

EVERYONE but RAFFAEL starts loosening their clothing.

RAFFAEL. Really, no! Amichichis! You cannot be serious!

LEO (*sings, sprawling all over the sofa*).
>Dibs on the couch!
>(*To* MARIANNE.) C'mon, babe, you and me on the couch...

CLAUDIA. I'll take the armchair.

PAUL. I'm fine on the floor.

FRITZ (*sings, to the* SOLDIER).
>I'm fine in your arms...

MUSIC continues underneath as THEY ALL settle in. RAFFAEL is incredulous and increasingly unnerved. The mixture of SINGING and RHYTHMIC DIALOGUE continues.

RAFFAEL.
>But Clowdia, what about your children?

CLAUDIA.
>What about them?

(*As* RAFFAEL *reacts:*)
We'll call. They'll be fine. Shiva's watching them.

RAFFAEL.
Shiva??

CLAUDIA.
The nanny, not the god.

MARIANNE.
Raffi, you stay too.

RAFFAEL.
Absurdo... No!

MUSIC STOPS. RAFFAEL *walks toward the portal to leave, then stops abruptly.*

Why not?!

RAFFAEL *undoes his tie preparatory to lying down near* CLAUDIA.

To sleep with a roomful of beautiful women? This is Utopia!

CLAUDIA. But no hanky-panky, Señoro!

RAFFAEL. Ah.

RAFFAEL *moves further off.*

WINDSOR. Lights out, ladies and gentlemen!

CLAUDIA. Hey, Windsor? Not *all* the lights, okay?

WINDSOR *leaves one light on. The* BISHOP, *finishing his prayers, lies down near* PAUL.

PAUL. Um. Your *hat*, Father?

BISHOP (*shifts his massive miter*). Oh. Sorry...

WINDSOR. Goodnight, Your Excellency.

RAFFAEL. And Windsor, we will want breakfast for nine.

WINDSOR (*seeing* McGOGG *is asleep*). Very good, sir. McGogg? *McGogg!*

RAFFAEL. No, it's fine. Let her be.

WINDSOR. Goodnight, Your Excellency.

WINDSOR *EXITS.*

LEO, *a bit drunk, hoists himself up from the couch, raises his glass and addresses the room.*

LEO (*sings*).
Ladies and gents,
Before 'Lights out',
Goodnight.
Sleep tight!

MARIANNE. Nightie-night, all!

ALL have now settled in. FRITZ *clings to the* SOLDIER.

SOLDIER. So. Our first night together.

FRITZ. Maybe our last. The last for everybody…

SOLDIER. Do you love me, Fritz? Truly love me?

FRITZ. Well – sure. Maybe. I mean, I don't really know you – and vice versa.

SOLDIER. I want to know everything about you. All your favorite things, your background. So tell me. Who are you?

FRITZ. Well, I was born in Greenwich.

SOLDIER. I was born in Spokane.

FRITZ. I like big cities…

SOLDIER. I love beaches.

FRITZ. I like some bustle, some energy.

SOLDIER. A nice long walk.

FRITZ. Demonstrations…

SOLDIER. Purple sunsets…

FRITZ. Old graveyards…

SOLDIER. Puppies.

FRITZ. I like places where… people work.

SOLDIER. Places that are beautiful.

FRITZ. ...places...

SOLDIER. ...places...

FRITZ. Not like this.

SOLDIER. Just like this.

FRITZ. This is the past.

SOLDIER. This is the past.

FRITZ. Who could live here?

SOLDIER. I could live here.

FRITZ. So anyway that's me, pretty much.

SOLDIER. I think we're made for each other.

FRITZ. Yes. *Yes*, we are, aren't we.

SOLDIER. I went in the army to experience real life. You're an experience.

FRITZ. Like – a good experience?

SOLDIER. Profound! Being with you is like – it's like crouching in a desert bunker on a moonless night.

FRITZ. Well, gosh.

SOLDIER. Yeah... Everything's quiet, everything's still. Can't see your fingers in front of your face. But you just know some bastard's out there waiting to get you. You start thinking maybe your time is up. Maybe it *is* up. Maybe you want it to be up. You want everything to just... *end.*

HE makes a SMALL EXPLOSION SOUND.

One stray mortar and –

HE makes a BIGGER EXPLOSION SOUND.

Intense, right?

HE MAKES A STILL BIGGER EXPLOSION SOUND.

That's you.

ACT TWO: THE ROOM

FRITZ. Y'know I haven't been out with many men, but this is a hell of a date.

SOLDIER. This isn't a *date*. This isn't some night out. Fritz, this is love. *Love*. And we're in it now! Do or die! Forever!

A DISTANT EXPLOSION FROM OUTSIDE. FRITZ reacts.

MUSIC RESUMES.

SOLDIER (*tenderly, sings*).   FRITZ (*sings frantically*).
    It's the end of the world…   It's the end of the world

SOLDIER.
    Yes, I know –

FRITZ.
    No, the actual
    End of the world!

ANOTHER DISTANT EXPLOSION. FRITZ covers her eyes in despair. MUSIC CONTINUES.

SOLDIER.
    Sounds like fireworks –

FRITZ (*speaks, in rhythm*).
    What am I doing here?

SOLDIER.
    Why are there fireworks?

FRITZ.
    It's Judgment Day. Chaos. Barricades.

ANOTHER DISTANT EXPLOSION.

SOLDIER.
    Let's go up on the terrace
    And watch.

FRITZ.
    I sort of like it right here.

SOLDIER.
    You do?

FRITZ.
    Don't you? I sort of like where we are.

SOLDIER.
>Me, too.

FRITZ.
>You do?

SOLDIER.
>I like wherever you are,
>I want to be wherever you are.
>I want to like whatever you like –
>Know what you know –
>See what you see.
>I want to get inside of you.

A BEAT.

FRITZ. So let's go in the closet and fuck!

SOLDIER. Yes! We can make love and then kill ourselves.

FRITZ. Why don't we see how the sex goes first?

SOLDIER.
>You are infinite!
>Is this just one of my dreams – ?
>Only a dream – ?
>I'm something of a dreamer.

FRITZ. Yes, I've noticed.

SOLDIER.
>But this is too surreal to be a dream.

>FRITZ *and the* SOLDIER *EXIT into the closet. The room is quiet for a moment. Then MUSIC BEGINS, as…*

Interlude 1

MARIANNE *sits up from her sleep.*

MARIANNE. What *was* it…?

>What in the world
>Was that Thing
>I was supposed to *do* today?!

>It's still there

Still floating
Just out of reach

Come on
Think
Marianne

Think think think

A BEAR CROSSES THROUGH THE ROOM. MARIANNE *doesn't notice.*

Oh, well.

I guess it's just gone

Poof!

And…

Poof!

And… Go to sleep, Marianne!

SHE LIES BACK DOWN. The BEAR RE-ENTERS and goes around sniffing people, growling a bit. MARIANNE *SITS BACK UP, not noticing the bear moving gradually toward her.*

The thing is

There have been so many moments
In my life
So many wonderful
Beautiful
Incandescent moments

When I thought

I am going to remember this

Forever

And now
I can't remember
A single one of them

Oh, well

Too late

They're gone

Sigh

SHE SIGHS.

And a deeper sigh

SHE SIGHS MORE DEEPLY.

And –

MARIANNE *finds her looking right into the face of the bear.*

God!!!

Who are you?

MARIANNE *takes the BEAR in her arms and waltzes with it.*

Remember *this*, Marianne

Remember this

And

(*Sings.*)
　Let it stay
　Just this way
　Forever

The BEAR whirls out of her arms and EXITS.

Yes, yes

I will remember this

And who knows

Maybe

I can still do
That other thing

That maddening mysterious thing

Whatever it was

Tomorrow…

MARIANNE *lies down and falls back into a deep sleep.*
The SCENE CHANGES TO…

Scene Two: The Same, Next Morning

EVERYONE is asleep. FRITZ *and the* SOLDIER *are still offstage.*

WINDSOR *bangs a loud gong.*

WINDSOR. Good morning! Did we all sleep well?

The GROUP stirs and wakes.

PAUL. I was dead out.

CLAUDIA. I didn't wake up even once.

MARIANNE. I didn't either. I slept like a child! (*Realizing.*) Oh, wait a moment!… No! I dreamt there was a bear in here…

LEO. It was probably your mother.

MARIANNE (*she's heard it many times before*). Ha, ha.

McGOGG *materializes with a cart with a coffee urn and some meagre food offerings.*

BISHOP (*waking in terror*). *Where am I, where am I?*

PAUL. It's okay. We're friends.

BISHOP. Sorry. That happens sometimes.

PAUL. Good morning, Colonel.

COL. MARTIN (*absent-mindedly*). Apparently… Yes, it is…

LEO (*groans, shivering audibly and violently*). Eugh… *Eugh…*

MARIANNE. Leo? Leo, what is it, darling?

LEO. I dunno. I feel like shit.

MARIANNE. You ate too much. And Mr Ulcer doesn't like that.

CLAUDIA. Breakfast! Yaaay!

EVERYONE *swarms the cart with cries of 'I'm starving', 'I'm famished', 'I could kill for coffee', etc. ALL grab food.*

BISHOP. Chocolate Danishes! *Yum yum.*

MARIANNE (*to* LEO). Not too much, darling, be kind to yourself. (*To* McGOGG, *at the coffee urn.*) May I have just a *soupçon* of coffee?

PAUL. Not much food here.

CLAUDIA. It looks like a lot of leftovers to me.

PAUL. *A jar of pickled herring?* Really?

LEO (*tapping the Danish to prove it*). This Danish is like a rock.

RAFFAEL *pulls* WINDSOR *aside.*

RAFFAEL. Windsor, what is all this? Where is breakfast?

WINDSOR. I'm sorry, sir. This is all we have. The deliveries didn't arrive and everyone is gone.

RAFFAEL. Gone? Who is gone, gone where?

WINDSOR. Brunnhilde. All the servants. I don't know where. They vanished in the night and cleaned out the pantry.

RAFFAEL. Ah-ha. This is that English sense of humor.

WINDSOR. No, it's reality, sir.

RAFFAEL. Reality? *Here?* Since when?

WINDSOR. Today.

BISHOP. That's funny…

PAUL. What's that, Bishop?

BISHOP. The piano died. Look at that.

BISHOP *idly hits various keys on the piano but gets no sound.*

Nothing… Not a note. Not even a whisper.

PAUL. How odd.

BISHOP. Ah, well – (*Blessing the piano.*) Rest in peace.

FRITZ *and the* SOLDIER *emerge from the closet.*

MARIANNE. Well, good morning, young lovers!

FRITZ. Ha, ha. (*To* SOLDIER.) Oh, God, don't look at me. I'm a trainwreck.

SOLDIER. You are the Orient Express of trainwrecks. You are –

FRITZ. Yeah, yeah, I'm the Acheson Topeka and the Santa Fe. What I am is hungry. Sorry. I'm often not nice in the morning.

SOLDIER. I'll remember – for all the rest of our mornings.

FRITZ (*to ALL*). Did anybody hear gunshots last night?

SOLDIER. The only thing I heard was us.

FRITZ. Right…

MARIANNE *is looking in a compact mirror.*

MARIANNE. I need to freshen up. Claudia?

CLAUDIA. Yeah, let's hit the powder room, pronto.

MARIANNE. Isn't this *fun*? And from now on, I'm never wearing *anything* but a negligee!

MARIANNE *and* CLAUDIA *approach the portal – and stop short. Distinct pause.*

MARIANNE. Oh, I don't really need to.   CLAUDIA. I'm fine, I'll fix me later.

MARIANNE *and* CLAUDIA *back off from the portal.*

PAUL. Hey, Windsor, you got any teaspoons?

WINDSOR. Of course, sir. Immediately, sir…

WINDSOR *heads for the portal but hesitates as he reaches it.*

COL. MARTIN. You heard the man, Windsor. He wants teaspoons.

WINDSOR *sinks into a chair near the portal.*

WINDSOR. I'm sorry. I suddenly feel a bit dizzy.

PAUL. Okay, *I'll* go find the damn teaspoons.

PAUL approaches the portal. Stops short.

But I can do without...

EVERYBODY continues chattering.

COL. MARTIN. Ladies and gentlemen, may I have your attention, please?

SOLDIER. Listen up!

EVERYBODY stops to listen.

COL. MARTIN. Has anyone in this room noticed anything unusual this morning?

MARIANNE. Anything unusual?

CLAUDIA. I haven't noticed anything.

LEO. Wait, what do you mean, unusual?

COL. MARTIN. I mean anything out of the ordinary? Anything weird, odd, strange, bizarre?

MARIANNE. Not me.

CLAUDIA. I haven't noticed anything.

PAUL. Me either.

BISHOP. The piano died.

COL. MARTIN. Bishop, I'm talking about a bigger picture here.

BISHOP. It seemed bizarre to me...

COL. MARTIN. May I point out that nobody has gone out of here this morning? Or last night? We have all stayed right here in this very room.

RAFFAEL. Well, of course we have! We were under the spell of good food – well, fairly good food – good company...

COL. MARTIN. Such good company you slept in here?

MARIANNE. Everybody likes a sleepover.

COL. MARTIN. On the floor? In your clothing? Why are we eating here instead of the dining room?

LEO. Say, what is all this?

COL. MARTIN. I challenge you – any of you – to walk across that threshold. Out of here, into there. How about you, Mr Brink?

LEO. Who, me? I can leave any time I want to. I'm just not feeling a hundred percent today.

COL. MARTIN. In other words, no. Padre, would you care to lead out the flock?

BISHOP. I'm in the middle of this Danish at the moment...

RAFFAEL. This is absurd! Windsor? You lead the way.

WINDSOR. Your Excellency, I certainly mayn't leave if you mayn't.

RAFFAEL. Well, I say you *may* leave.

WINDSOR. And I must beg your indulgence not to.

RAFFAEL. Then I command you to leave. Now!

COL. MARTIN. I think you've proved my point. Ladies and gentlemen, I put it to you: I say nobody has left this room... because we *can't*.

A small pause.

MARIANNE. I just got a little *frisson*!

PAUL. Well, heck, just call in the help! They'll come and rescue us!

MARIANNE. Isn't that why we call them *help*?

RAFFAEL. Actually, there is no help. The servants ran off last night.

CLAUDIA. Ran off? What do you mean *ran off*? You mean abandoned us?

COL. MARTIN. Why would that be, sir?

RAFFAEL. I don't know. They must have had some reason for… abandoning us…

CLAUDIA. They knew something, that's why. And now we're in here all alone?

MARIANNE. Without a staff?

CLAUDIA. Yeah, like I say. ALONE?

PAUL. Easy, Claude, easy.

BISHOP. So we can't leave…

LEO (*taking out his phone*). Kids, kids! I'll take care of this. I got a Mr Fixer, he'll be here in no time…

CLAUDIA (*taking out her phone*). I'm calling Shiva.

LEO. Whoa whoa whoa. My phone is dead.

EVERYBODY reaches for phones.

PAUL. You're kidding…

BISHOP. Dead?

FRITZ (*more or less to herself*). Of course they're dead.

CLAUDIA. I've got the new Twenty-Five, that's not going to… *My phone is dead!* OH MY GOD, MY PHONE IS DEAD!

BISHOP. What in *hell* is going on here?!

RAFFAEL. Please, please! Mimis amichichis! Not to worry! It's not as if we are under some kind of curse here, or a magic spell. This is not a sorcerer's castle.

CLAUDIA. You're the one who got us into this, you invited us here!

PAUL. Calm down, honey.

CLAUDIA. We're rats on a sinking ship. On your ship, Raffi. You brought us into this trap!

RAFFAEL. By opening my doors to you? You were all delighted!

ACT TWO: THE ROOM   81

LEO. Yeah, delighted till I got stomach poisoning! Now I'm sweating like a pig here and I can't *leave*?

CLAUDIA. We could *DIE* in here! Thanks to you!

RAFFAEL. Clowdia, please, I am not your enemy!

CLAUDIA. Well, then, who is? Who did this to us and what do they want?

CLAUDIA runs to the portal and shouts out of it:

WHAT DO YOU WANT? WHAT DO YOU WANT? *JUST TELL US WHAT YOU WANT!*

Her words ECHO in the emptiness of the Embassy.

PAUL. Honey… Claude…

PAUL puts his arms around her. CLAUDIA starts to cry quietly.

CLAUDIA. I'm sorry. I'm sorry.

BISHOP. My friends, may I just say one word here? *Providence.* Whatever's happening to us here, and I have no bloody idea what it is, there is a reason for all this.

LEO. Hey. St. Francis. Last I heard, you were going door to door looking for a job. We're in a situation here, we gotta *act*.

PAUL. Colonel Martin, what do we do?

COL. MARTIN. What we do is, we *make* do. And to make do, we do *without*.

CLAUDIA. Without what?

COL. MARTIN. Everything – if we're going to survive. (*The breakfast cart:*) Here's our canteen. We've still got some java. We can ration out the Danishes and the pickled herring. That vase is a water source. The chrysanthemums will provide valuable protein.

MARIANNE. They're gladioli.

COL. MARTIN. Lieutenant, commandeer those flowers.

SOLDIER. Yes, sir!

BISHOP. What are we supposed to do about, you know, bathrooms?

COLONEL MARTIN *picks up the CHINESE JAR.*

COL. MARTIN. Here's your bathroom. The closet will do for privacy.

HE hands a jar to the SOLDIER, *who takes it into the closet.*

MARIANNE. Privacy for what?

COL. MARTIN. Doing your duty.

MARIANNE. That's a Ming jar!

COL. MARTIN. It's a Ming toilet now.

CLAUDIA. So we're doomed. We're doomed!

RAFFAEL. Clowdia. Everyone. Please! It is not so bad! We are in a beautiful place, we're safe, we're among friends…

LEO. Yeah, great friend, Raffi. First you come over for some mythical brunch I never heard of. Then you feed me carrots with ptomaine sauce. I didn't have to come here. I coulda gone to the office and made myself useful! I coulda flown to Paris and had a *real* meal! I coulda gone to a brothel and gotten *laid*, for God's sake!

BISHOP. Well good, we're expressing some feelings.

MARIANNE. Wait, wait, wait. Did you say *brothel*?!

LEO. Yeah, I said brothel.

MARIANNE. You go to *BROTHELS*?

LEO. Yes. I go to brothels. Okay? I go to very *GOOD* brothels!

RAFFAEL. You know, many men still go to br–

MARIANNE. I'm not talking to you! I'm talking to *you*. *A BROTHEL?*

LEO (*falling to the floor, choking*). A BROTHEL? *GAAAAAAAHHHHHHHHHHHH!*

MARIANNE. Oh, very funny, Leo.

LEO. *GAAAAAAAAAAAAAAHHHHHH!*

MARIANNE. Yes, the old routine. Hilarious!

LEO. Help me… Help me…!

LEO *writhes and chokes on the floor.*

RAFFAEL. I do not think he is joking.

CLAUDIA. Paul, what is this?

PAUL. I don't know.

CLAUDIA. You're a doctor, you don't *know*?

PAUL. I'm not a doctor, I'm a plastic surgeon! – Leo! Leo, do you know where you are?

LEO *moans.*

Do you know the President's name?

LEO *moans louder.*

Do you know what you ate last night?

LEO. Beef Bordelaise.

PAUL. Good, he's conscious.

LEO. I'm so cold, I'm so goddamn cold.

PAUL. Give him some brandy.

COL. MARTIN. We're going to have to ration the liquor –

CLAUDIA. Give him some goddam brandy!

LEO (*groans in pain*). Oh God. Oh God…

PAUL (*to* WINDSOR). Come on, asshole, don't just stand there!

RAFFAEL. Windsor, give him the brandy.

WINDSOR. Actually, Your Excellency… Under the circumstances –

WINDSOR *drops the perfect manservant and the English accent.*

I don't gotta do *nothin'*. Stuff it up your ass. All a you!

RAFFAEL. Windsor – you're not *English*?!

WINDSOR. Oh my gosh, *appearance and reality, appearance and reality*! FUCK YOU! And by the way the name is Inferno.

RAFFAEL. I *beg* your pardon?

WINDSOR. INFERNO. I AM INFERNO! I AM YOUR WORST NIGHTMARE!

PAUL. Well, can you pour us a brandy, Inferno?

WINDSOR. Sure I can. For a hundred bucks I can.

PAUL. *What?!*

WINDSOR. You want anything offa this cart – which is now *my* cart – it's gonna cost you a hundred bucks.

PAUL *makes a move toward the cart.* WINDSOR *takes out a pistol and* PAUL *stops in his tracks.*

Cash.

COLONEL MARTIN *reaches for his gun and realizes it's in* WINDSOR*'s hand.*

COL. MARTIN. You dog!

WINDSOR. You want a Danish offa my *food cart* here? Two hundred.

COL. MARTIN. This is black marketeering!

WINDSOR. No, this is laissez faire economics. I'm the laissez. You're the faire.

RAFFAEL. But Windsor – and I *will* call you Windsor – this is your gratitude?

WINDSOR. For what? For being your lackey? I'm supposed to say 'Thank you' for herding me around like a sheep? Well now all you people, *you're* the sheep.

PAUL (*offering cash from his wallet*). Fine, fine, *here*, just give me a brandy.

WINDSOR. What is that?

ACT TWO: THE ROOM   85

PAUL. You want money, it's money.

WINDSOR. Didn't I just tell you what you are? Remind me. It starts with 'S-H.' What are you again?

PAUL. I'm, um… I'm a sheep.

WINDSOR. Good! So what do you say to me? Mister-Sheep-who-wants-a-brandy?

PAUL. 'Please' – ?

WINDSOR. What is 'please'? *In sheep language.*

PAUL. I'm not going to –

WINDSOR *fires the pistol in the air.*

WINDSOR. What you say, sheep? Lemme hear it.

PAUL. Baaaaaaa.

WINDSOR. Excuse me?

PAUL. *BAAAAAAA!*

WINDSOR. Beautiful. Now I wanna hear it from Mrs Sheep.

CLAUDIA. I represent a major entertainment entity –

WINDSOR. No you don't. You're a crap agent for mid-level nobodies. AND I AM YOUR SHEPHERD! What do you say?

CLAUDIA. Baaaaaaa.

WINDSOR (*to* RAFFAEL). Now you, jerkoff.

RAFFAEL. I refuse. I am going to retain my dignity.

WINDSOR *puts the gun to* RAFFAEL*'s head.*

Baaaaaaa.

WINDSOR. Everybody! Come on!

EVERYBODY ELSE BUT FRITZ. BAAAAAAA!

WINDSOR. And again, LOUDER!

EVERYBODY ELSE BUT FRITZ. *BAAAAAAA!*

MARIANNE. I've never done that before.

WINDSOR. And you rich bastards thought you done everything! Now loud and clear! Everybody!

EVERYBODY INCLUDING FRITZ. BAAAAAAA!

WINDSOR. A-plus. Your brandy, Mr Sheep.

DISTANT GUNSHOTS are heard. EVERYBODY goes silent.

CLAUDIA. What was that?

FRITZ. I told you. It's the end of the world.

MARIANNE. Yes, but *today*?

FRITZ (*to* WINDSOR). Today?

WINDSOR. Today.

MARIANNE. But, Colonel, if it's the end of the world – what do we do?

COL. MARTIN. Traditionally, Mrs Brink, there are no options.

LOUD GUNSHOTS and EXPLOSIONS heard.

THEY ALL stare into the void. Frozen, speechless, completely still. Shock. Fear. Loss. Anger.

LIGHTS GO DOWN ON THEM like that…

Interlude 2

MUSIC as LIGHTS COME UP and we see them in the middle of the night, wandering around room… lost…

LIGHTS CHANGE. MUSIC CONTINUES.

Time has passed. McGOGG *heads for the portal.*

SOLDIER. *STAY AWAY FROM THE PERIMETER, PLEASE!*

FRITZ. Easy, babe. Easy…

McGOGG *moves away from the portal.*

LIGHTS CHANGE. More time passes. They are all still wandering the room.

MUSIC ENDS.

THE SCENE CHANGES abruptly as the LIGHTS SNAP UP.

Scene Three: The Same

The room and their clothes have deteriorated a bit. LEO *ails on the couch.* CLAUDIA *power-walks around the edges of the room.*

McGOGG *dusts.* WINDSOR *makes cats' cradles.*

MARIANNE, FRITZ, RAFFAEL, COLONEL MARTIN, BISHOP *and* PAUL *are playing charades. THE* SOLDIER *times them.*

SOLDIER. One minute. And – *GO!*

MARIANNE (*fumfering*). Um um um – OKAY!

    MARIANNE *starts miming her clue for* PAUL *and* RAFFAEL.

PAUL. All right, two words. Two words, five syllables.

BISHOP. Are we ahead, who's winning?

COL. MARTIN. Shhhhhhh!

PAUL. Keep going, Mare!

    MARIANNE *does the charade sign for 'book'.*

RAFFAEL. It's a film!

PAUL. No, it means a book, famous book.

    MARIANNE *does the 'big idea' sign.*

Okay now, big idea. Big idea.

RAFFAEL. *Don Quixote!*

PAUL. She hasn't done anything yet! Go ahead, Mare.

    MARIANNE *mimes poling a river raft.*

RAFFAEL. *Crime and Punishment*! *Pride and Prejudice*! *Antony and Cleopatra*!

LEO. *Two words*, Raffi! For God's sake!

SOLDIER. No kibitzing!

RAFFAEL. Crime and punishment is two words…

MARIANNE *poles harder.*

PAUL. You're doing Pilates. You're harvesting wheat. You're… sweeping a floor very slowly…

BISHOP (*waving his hand*). I know what it is! I know what it is!

FRITZ (*pulling the* BISHOP*'s hand down*). We're on the other team.

The BISHOP *whispers the answer in the* COLONEL*'s ear.*

CLAUDIA (*shouts, power-walking around them*). I'm VERY HUNGRY!

MARIANNE *keeps poling but now makes water sounds.*

SOLDIER. No sound effects!

RAFFAEL. You are having sex! Are you having some kind of sex?

LEO. You morons.

MARIANNE. Ignore the man on the sofa!

PAUL. Keep going, Mare!

SOLDIER. Thirty seconds.

BISHOP. This is exciting.

MARIANNE *fans her face.*

RAFFAEL. Heat. Lots of heat. You're hot, God, you are so hot!

PAUL. Menopause! Hot flashes!

MARIANNE. *I am poling a RAFT on the MISSISSIPPI!*

FRITZ. HEY!

ACT TWO: THE ROOM 89

RAFFAEL. 'Poling a raft on the Mississippi'…?

PAUL. Never mind! Act out the words, do the words.

MARIANNE *mimes picking berries off a bush and eating them.*

Okay. Eating something. Cherries. Picking cherries.

RAFFAEL. *The Red and the Black*!

MARIANNE *waves her arms like fins.*

PAUL. Um, wings. Wings. Bird. *To Kill a Mockingbird*.

MARIANNE *moves her lips like a fish.*

Fish! Fins! Okay, *fins*. Um.

RAFFAEL. *Finnegans Wake*!

PAUL. *Jaws*! *Moby-Dick*! *The Old Man and the Sea*!

SOLDIER. Time!

PAUL. MOTHERFUCK!

The BISHOP *applauds.* MARIANNE *collapses with a groan.*

COL. MARTIN. One more point for our side.

WINDSOR. *Huckleberry Finn*. You illiterates.

RAFFAEL. What is a huckleberry finn? Well, basta! A stupid game…

COL. MARTIN. You can't quit the game! We're winning!

PAUL. Hey Leo, you want to play?

MARIANNE. *No*. The game is over. But really. *Huckleberry FINN*!?

PAUL. So shoot me.

CLAUDIA (*stops power-walking, breathless*). Ten thousand.

PAUL. I'm gonna hit the Ming.

PAUL *goes into the closet.*

FRITZ. Well, that was a distraction. At least.

BISHOP (*intoning*). 'Distracted from distraction by distraction'!

LEO. Jesus Christ...

BISHOP. T. S. Eliot, actually.

THEY shift about restlessly, from time to time pausing at the portal and looking out at us.

WINDSOR *creeps up on* FRITZ.

WINDSOR (*quietly to* FRITZ). Nice to see you're having fun, *Apocalypse*.

FRITZ. Shhhh!

WINDSOR *moves away.*

BISHOP (*mimes playing, humming* MARIANNE*'s tune*). Dum dum dum dummmmm... What day is it today? Is it Thursday?

LEO. It's yesterday. Or the day before.

RAFFAEL (*quietly to* CLAUDIA). Perhaps it is a 'Tuesday'...

CLAUDIA. Oh, please. In *here*?

BISHOP. It certainly *feels* like a Thursday.

CLAUDIA. *IS IT IMPORTANT*? I'm HUNGRY.

MARIANNE. There is the old cliché. To think about the starving children of China.

CLAUDIA. Yeah, *think* about them, not *be* them. But thank you for the thought, Miss I'm-Never-Going-To-Wear-Anything-But-This-Negligee. (*Belts* MARIANNE*'s words, mockingly.*) 'I wanna live in this ROOM! I wanna live in this GODDAMN *ROOOOOM*!'

RAFFAEL. The last cigarette.

He lights it very slowly, savoring it.

PAUL *enters from the closet as* CLAUDIA *takes out her* (*dead*) *phone and starts pounding.*

PAUL. What are you doing? Honey?

CLAUDIA. I'm calling the kids. (*Into her phone.*) JOSHUA! ABBY! Come to the phone! It's me, it's Mom!

PAUL. Claudia…

CLAUDIA (*into her phone*). I miss you so much, so so much…

PAUL. Claude, your phone is dead.

PAUL *gently takes the phone away from her.*

CLAUDIA. But – what if *they* are, too? How would we know?

PAUL. I hear you, honey.

CLAUDIA. Well, screw you, Paul! *Where is everybody? Why doesn't somebody come for us?*

BISHOP. People may not even know we're here.

CLAUDIA. Maybe there is nobody. Maybe we're the only survivors.

MARIANNE. I wonder how the dogs are doing.

PAUL. Which ones? The real ones or the copies?

MARIANNE. They're all real –

PAUL. *What were you two thinking?* I mean, have they all MET? And how do you think they're going to feel when they do? Looking in a mirror of *themselves*, these duplicate poodles?

LEO. *Paul, nobody is cloned yet.* Okay? There has been no procedure. Everybody is real till further notice.

PAUL. Fine.

LEO (*on the couch, weakly*). Can I have some water? Marianne? Some water?

MARIANNE *pointedly ignores* LEO, *studying her nails.*

MARIANNE (*hums*). 'Are we not blessed…?'

FRITZ (*to* SOLDIER). What do you say? A drink of water for Leo?

SOLDIER. I'm not authorized to make that decision.

FRITZ. Come on! He needs water. He's sick.

SOLDIER. Colonel?

COL. MARTIN. Permission granted. But not too much of that.

SOLDIER hands the vase to FRITZ.

FRITZ. Such a boy scout…

She gives the vase to LEO.

Here you go. Drink up.

LEO (*smelling the water before drinking*). Eugh. Disgusting.

MARIANNE regards her now-thoroughly-wilted WHITE ROSE.

MARIANNE. Oh, well. I knew it had to happen sometime…

SHE SLOWLY EATS THE WHITE ROSE. CLAUDIA and PAUL gather to watch, fascinated by the sight of food.

So beautiful and so delicate, it smells so wonderful – and it tastes just *awful*!

PAUL. It looks fantastic.

MARIANNE (*still eating*). It's inedible. I swear. Absolutely disgusting.

MARIANNE finishes the rose, sighing.

PAUL goes to WINDSOR at the food cart, which is covered.

PAUL. What've you got today, Inferno?

WINDSOR. I'm on a break. Come back later.

PAUL. My wife is hungry, I'm *asking* what you *have*.

WINDSOR. What're you gonna give me for it? You're outa cash.

PAUL (*offering his watch*). Okay. My Patek Philippe.

WINDSOR. Terrific. Now I can count every pico-second I'm stuck in a room with you parasites. Go away.

PAUL. You know what I think? I think you're cleaned out. *Are you cleaned out, asshole?*

PAUL *pushes* WINDSOR *aside and uncovers the cart. No food.*

Empty. Nothing.

CLAUDIA. Nothing…? Wait. You mean – *nothing*?

LEO. Out of business, huh. That's fucking hilarious. Welcome to the have-nots – '*Inferno*'.

WINDSOR (*holds up the GUN*). I still have this.

LEO. Yeah. The last resort of nobodies.

WINDSOR. I'm just as good as you!

LEO. If you're as good as me, how come you're in a duck suit, cleaning people's toilets for a living?

WINDSOR. Don't you talk to me like that!

LEO. Yeah, what're you gonna do?

WINDSOR *points the gun at* LEO *and cocks it. EVERYBODY notices.*

WINDSOR. Don't tempt me!

FRITZ. No. NO! Stop it. Stop. That's enough!

FRITZ *pushes the pointed gun in another direction. A TENSE SILENCE in the room. Nobody knows what's going to happen.*

WINDSOR. Okay… (*Suddenly holds the gun out to* FRITZ.) You do it.

FRITZ. What…?

WINDSOR. You want to end oppression? There's the king. Shoot the bastard, Apocalypse!

SOLDIER. 'Apocalypse'…?

WINDSOR. Oh my goodness, no. Little Fritzie? An agent for PRADA?

BISHOP. Not the *shoe*...?

MARIANNE (*shushing him, scared*). Not the shoe, not the shoe.

WINDSOR (*to FRITZ, offering the gun again*). Take it!

FRITZ. No.

WINDSOR. I didn't think so. You see what you are? Unnecessary. (*Spoken, pointing the gun at each in turn.*) BANG, BANG, BANG, BANG, BANG!

THEY wait in scared silence for what might come next.

(*Grandly, to the room.*) The only reason you're still here is I love to see you suffer.

WINDSOR *retreats to his corner. EVERYONE regroups. It felt like a close call.*

FRITZ *realizes the* SOLDIER *is staring at her with hostility.*

FRITZ. Listen, can I explain? Please?

SOLDIER. Leave me alone.

FRITZ. Can I at least *try*?

SOLDIER. *Leave me alone!*

SOLDIER *leaves* FRITZ *standing.*

BISHOP. Alone might be difficult...

MARIANNE *touches* FRITZ's *arm.*

MARIANNE. Fritzie...

FRITZ *shakes her off.*

The group wanders the room again.

COLONEL MARTIN *regards the portal in frustration.*

COL. MARTIN. There's got to be a solution. Some way out of here. We haven't all gone crazy!

FRITZ *stands regarding* LEO, *who is very still, his eyes closed.*

LEO (*eyes still closed*). Stop staring at me.

FRITZ. Sorry. I thought you were…

LEO *turns to her and opens his eyes.*

LEO. Dead? You know, I don't mind dying. But not like this, in a crowd of people. She ever gonna talk to me again?

FRITZ. She's just being Marianne. You know. Pastel cast-iron.

LEO. So. You happy now? You satisfied? You got what you wanted. You wanted us on our knees. You got that – *and then some*. Take a picture, why dontcha. 'Apocalypse'?

FRITZ. Leo, whatever I did I was acting on –

LEO. *Principles*. Oh, sure, sure. Everybody here's got those. But you know, kid, torching stuff is easy. Incinerate the world? Piece of cake. You just better have some idea what you're gonna build with the ashes.

FRITZ. Your world has to go.

LEO. And you think *I'm* ruthless.

FRITZ. Well, you exploited people for years and years!

LEO. At least I'm not a hypocrite. Sucking the tit of the bourgeoisie while bitching about 'em. Those nice people who took you out to dinner ten times a month? You know what you are, you're like your cheeseburger: pink around the edges. Now go on, get lost. You're making me sicker than I am.

FRITZ – *stung – moves away from* LEO.

(*As* FRITZ *moves off*:) But thanks for revving me up a little! Comrade!

RAFFAEL *slips away from the group, takes out his pocketwatch, opens it, and is about to sample some white powder…*

PAUL. Hey. What are you doing?

RAFFAEL. Shhhhh!

PAUL. I want some of that! Or give it to Leo. He could use it.

RAFFAEL. Leo is on his way to meet Mama Muerte. But I will happily give you a pinch. What is it worth to you?

PAUL. Worth to me?! Those are *my* drugs! *Partly* my drugs.

CLAUDIA *comes over to them.*

CLAUDIA. What are you two conspiring about? What is that?

CLAUDIA *grabs the watch and spills the cocaine.*

PAUL / RAFFAEL. *NO!*

RAFFAEL. Do you realize what you just did? You ignorant woman?

MARIANNE *joins them and looks on drolly.*

MARIANNE. Claudia, you just spilled about fifty thousand semolinas worth of pumpkin.

CLAUDIA. Pumpkin is *cocaine*?

PAUL. Shhh!

CLAUDIA. Yeah? Who's gonna hear? *Besides me?*

COLONEL MARTIN *has overheard the last of this, and interrupts.*

COL. MARTIN. Excuse me, excuse me. *You're* the cartel?

RAFFAEL. Guilty! Yes! We are the cartel! And what will you do about it, Co-lo-nel?

COL. MARTIN. Well, you can consider yourselves under house arrest.

RAFFAEL. We *ARE* under house arrest! *In my house!*

MARIANNE. Bordellos, drug cartels, the things one learns in life.

LEO. Can I have some water, please?

BISHOP. Nothing here. All out.

PAUL. There's no *water*…?

He turns the vase over. It's empty.

ACT TWO: THE ROOM   97

FRITZ. Well, *Kommandant*. People are thirsty in here. What are you doing about it?

COL. MARTIN. Well…

FRITZ. We have no options, is that what you're going to tell me? That's not good enough anymore. (*Starts chanting.*) WA-TER! WA-TER! WA-TER!

COL. MARTIN. I'm sorry! I can't help you!

FRITZ. You're telling *me*?

FRITZ / CLAUDIA / MARIANNE. WA-TER! WA-TER! WA-TER!

The chants get louder and bigger. During that, McGOGG *quietly gets up and goes to a wall, taking the* BISHOP*'s crozier with her.*

FRITZ / CLAUDIA / MARIANNE / PAUL / BISHOP. *WA-TER! WA-TER! WA-TER!*

COL. MARTIN (*under the chant*). We cannot panic! There's nothing worse than panic! Please! Listen to me! This situation can't go on indefinitely!

McGOGG *strikes the wall with the crozier. The SOUND stops the chant.*

McGOGG *strikes the wall again with the crozier, and… WATER sprays out of the wall.*

ALL AD LIB CRIES OF JOY.

THEY rush in to get a drink. McGOGG *quietly goes and sits back down.*

Form a line, form a line! One at a time, please!

COLONEL MARTIN *pushes in to get his drink, too.*

RAFFAEL. Ha, ha, ha! What did I tell you? Life is good, mimis amichichis! La vidida ay estada el tidada!

THEY all dance in the waterfall.

After they've drunk their water and celebrated, the LIGHTS CHANGE TO NIGHT. THEY all disperse around the room.

A CAMPFIRE appears where the SOLDIER *was piling the firewood.*

MUSIC.

Interlude 3

Middle of the night. The BISHOP, *near the bookshelves, nibbles LITTLE WHITE SCRAPS heaped in the palm of his hand. He has a candle burning in a holder near him.*

MARIANNE *finds him.*

MARIANNE. What is that,
 What are you eating…?

BISHOP. Just a little midnight snack.

MARIANNE. Popcorn?

BISHOP. No, it's paper.

MARIANNE. *Paper*. Really…

BISHOP. And here we have this magnificent library.
 A feast!
 Try some, it's good.

 MARIANNE *cautiously takes a scrap.*

 It'll fool your stomach, anyway.

MARIANNE. That really *is* quite tasty!

BISHOP (*shows TORN-UP BOOK*). This is *A Tale of Two Cities*.

MARIANNE. I love *A Tale of Two Cities*! May I?

BISHOP. The classics.
 Always nourishing –
 Now literally so.

MARIANNE. Can I tell you a secret?

BISHOP. Of course.

MARIANNE. It's my birthday.

ACT TWO: THE ROOM   99

BISHOP. Today?

MARIANNE. Or somewhere *around* my birthday...

BISHOP. Mazel tov!
  But why is that a secret?

MARIANNE. Well, Leo never remembers...
  But isn't that a *sign*?
  Here we are, all together,
  Lots of time on our hands,
  This should be our chance to dig in!
  To talk about *real* things,
  Important things!
  Existence! The meaning of life!
  Isn't that why you came to the door?
  To discuss just that?

BISHOP. Yes, but... *the meaning of life*.
  Not that it's not important...

MARIANNE. Okay – so – not the meaning of life.
  What is... I don't know...
  Being, for example,
  According to the experts?

BISHOP. *Being*... 'Being.' Yes.

MARIANNE. Philosophically.

BISHOP. Ummmmmmm.

MARIANNE. What's the matter?

BISHOP. If I explain Being
  Will you let me hold your shoes?

MARIANNE. Of course!

  MARIANNE *takes off her shoes and gives them to the* BISHOP, *who holds them affectionately.*

  Go ahead, Father.
  I'm all agog.

BISHOP. Yes. Being. Well,
  First of all –

You might say –
We're here.
Actually *here*! On earth.
Most likely. Though perhaps not.
As are other people
And also objects –
Like these beautiful satin slippers.

MARIANNE. Yes? And?

BISHOP. And that *means* something.
That we're here.
We mean something, apparently.
We are what you might call
Matter that matters.
Or not. Depending on who you read.
So we're here
On, possibly, earth,
For a time
With these very soft satin slippers
And other people
Et cetera
And we live our lives
And then we
Die
And spend eternity with God –
Or go to hell
If there happens to be one
Or else we pass into complete nothingness,
A total void
Forever and ever
That we're actually unaware of
Because we're not here anymore
The End.

MARIANNE. I really enjoyed that.
What a world, hmmm?
With *Being*, and everything!

BISHOP (*giving the shoes back*).
Thank you for these.
Quite inspiring.

It begins to snow in the room.

MARIANNE. And look at that.
Snow.

BISHOP. Yes.
Or manna.

MARIANNE. Manna!
Without us even having ordered it!

BISHOP. Supposedly
That's how it works.
(*Checking one on his hand.*)
No. Definitely snow.

MARIANNE. So – just to be clear –
If all of that is '*Being*',
What are we supposed to do
About it?

BISHOP. I suppose –
Be here.
Until we're not.

MARIANNE. To be continued!

BISHOP. Exactly!
'To be' / continued
Until otherwise notified.

MARIANNE. No, I meant –
Well, maybe I did mean that!

MARIANNE *kisses the* BISHOP *on the cheek.*

Thank you, Father. Nightie-night!

BISHOP *takes the candle out of the holder and sets it on a book.*

BISHOP. Mrs Brink…

He presents the book and candle to her like a birthday cake.

Happy birthday. Make a wish.

MARIANNE *blows out the candle. BLACKOUT.*

Scene Four: The Same

The room and their clothes have deteriorated further. THEY look bedraggled and spacey, moving about as if in a dream. LEO *dozes restlessly on the couch.*

MARIANNE *brushes her hair at the mirror over and over again.*

CLAUDIA *sits huddled by herself in one corner. We can't see yet what she's doing.*

As they wander the room, COLONEL MARTIN *brushes against* RAFFAEL.

COL. MARTIN. Eugh...

RAFFAEL. Excuse me? Did you say something?

COL. MARTIN. I didn't say anything.

RAFFAEL. Yes. You said '*eugh*'. I distinctly heard you say 'eugh'.

COL. MARTIN. Small wonder. You stink, sir.

RAFFAEL. Oh, *I* stink. And you? You do not smell? Co-lo-*nel*?

BISHOP. Gentlemen...

RAFFAEL. Maybe I smell of rats, and rat-holes.

COL. MARTIN. Among other things.

MARIANNE. Will you two *stop*? I'm trying to brush my hair.

Silence.

COLONEL MARTIN *and* SOLDIER *have been quietly conferring.* SOLDIER *now starts breaking up a chair over his knee.*

FRITZ (*to the* SOLDIER). Hey, what're you doing? Where're we supposed to sit?

COL. MARTIN. It'll be cold again tonight. We'll need a fire.

FRITZ. Yeah, but that's, like, my chair...

SOLDIER. Just following orders.

MARIANNE. My arms are like tree branches.

The SOLDIER *tosses the chair-pieces into a pile of kindling.*
The BISHOP *presses down keys of the piano. No sound.*

CLAUDIA. Is that clock ticking faster? It is. It's ticking faster. You hear it?

WINDSOR. 'Scuse me.

WINDSOR *takes out the pistol and shoots the clock.*
LEO *sits up with a cry, startled.*

CLAUDIA (*goes back to what she'd been doing*). Thank you.

LEO. The fuck was that?

WINDSOR. It was me.

LEO. I thought I was dead, six feet under, only – somebody up there was standing on my grave shooting at me through the dirt...

WINDSOR. That would be me, too.

PAUL. So, Colonel, how long *does* it take a person to starve to death?

COL. MARTIN. As I understand it...

MARIANNE. *We're not discussing it, thank you.*

SOLDIER (*to* PAUL). Stand up, please, sir.

PAUL. What...

SOLDIER. I said STAND UP! This does not go there, this goes *here*. And this goes here. And this goes here. *Order*, you understand?

The SOLDIER *aggressively re-arranges the room.*

PAUL. What's all this?

CLAUDIA. I'm writing a letter to the kids. I hope they can read my writing. Have they ever seen my writing? Not important. (*Clears her throat, reads.*) 'My darling Abby, my darling Josh.'

She pauses a moment, goes on.

'I might be dead by now.'

PAUL. Clau…

CLAUDIA. 'So I'm writing this to tell you how much I love you – and how much I will always love you. I can't be there for you right now…' (*Revises, writing it in.*) '…or ever… so there's one thing I ask of you. Please, please, never be afraid. Of anything. Whatever you're afraid of, whatever monster, the thing in the basement, it's not going to look like what you thought anyway, you just be strong and you will conquer it. Also important: Abigail, I want you to have my chinchilla jacket.'

PAUL. STOP.

CLAUDIA. 'Never mind what the crazies say about fur.'

PAUL (*takes the letter away*). Just stop this right! Okay?

CLAUDIA. 'Wear it and enjoy it – ' (*Underlines.*) 'without fear.'

She loses it for a moment, collects herself.

PAUL. I'm ripping this up.

CLAUDIA. How much of my life have I wasted on the phone checking the grosses in *Variety*. Now I get to waste the *end* of my life in here?

PAUL. Try vacuuming cellulite. Or moving somebody's navel so their bikini looks better. Or making a thousand noses so everybody can look like everybody else. Don't tell *me* about wasting your life.

RAFFAEL. Oh, please! You think you wasted your life? I wanted to do something noble, I wanted make a mark in the world. What is my mark? Sex with four thousand, seven hundred and sixty-eight women!

BISHOP. Good Lord.

WINDSOR. I wanted the end of the world.

CLAUDIA. At least you got your wish.

WINDSOR. *No, I did not get my wish.* You're still here. I'm still here. Years and years trying to accomplish something, working to exterminate you types. Futility, boys and girls. Totally futile.

McGOGG (*Irish accent*). Ye know what?

Everybody stops and looks at McGOGG.

I've actually had quite a good life.

Simultaneous:

MARIANNE. As a maid, really?
CLAUDIA. Oh, well, *that's wonderful*!
PAUL. How very nice for you!
RAFFAEL. You are fired, you hear me?
FRITZ. Perfect. Perfect!
COL. MARTIN. Oh, come *on*.

LEO *speaks up now, standing on the couch.*

LEO. Well, I say FUCK YOU ALL. Grow up. You know what? I've wasted my life and I say so-the-fuck-what. Don't tell me about the meaning of life. Non-itemized credit derivatives? Are they meaningful? No! Did they make me a lotta money? Yeah, and I say *bring 'em on*. I'm gonna die and go to hell? Bring that on, too! I'll take over hell and turn it into condos!

FRITZ. Leo, you're feverish.

LEO. No, I'm not. I'm *sane*. And I do not apologize for ANYTHING! I say screw this stinking world, I say screw this filthy universe. I'm just glad I won't be here to see the extermination. The hell with food! The hell with friends! The hell with restaurants and menus and Beef Bordelaise! The hell with it all!

LEO *wobbles, out of breath, staring at them fixedly.*

PAUL (*confidentially to the others*). Guys – this sounds serious.

MARIANNE (*skeptically*). Oh, yes, I'm sure.

> LEO *collapses suddenly. ALL except* MARIANNE *rush to him.*

FRITZ. What is it, Paul, what's happening?

PAUL (*sotto voce, to them all*). It's bad. It's really bad.

MARIANNE. Oh, please.

LEO. Marianne. Talk to me. Just let me hear your voice. One word, that's all I want.

> MARIANNE *remains staunchly silent.*

BISHOP. Mrs Brink… I know you're angry –

MARIANNE. I have nothing to say to that man. He is not sick, he is not dying, he's just a great big *baby*.

COL. MARTIN. Padre, you want to take over here?

BISHOP. Um, yes. My children, would you all give us a moment?

LEO. No, no. I'm not ashamed. Let 'em listen in.

BISHOP. Is there anything you want to say to anyone here, Leo?

LEO. Yeah. Tell my wife I love her.

> MARIANNE *just scoffs and turns away.*

BISHOP. All right, yes, very good.

LEO. Tell her if I was going anywhere, she's the only thing I'd miss out of this whole stinking asshole of a world.

BISHOP. I can certainly pass that on. Anything else? Last inspirational thoughts on life?

LEO. I made my first trade on twenty-six dollars.

BISHOP. I don't mean business life.

LEO. No, this is important. When I was fifteen I broke into a house on Marquette Avenue in Utica and I killed two people.

COL. MARTIN. Wait wait wait wait wait. You killed two people…

LEO. In Utica, New York.

COL. MARTIN. On Marquette Avenue?

LEO. With a Smith & Wesson.

COL. MARTIN. For twenty-six dollars?

LEO. And fifteen cents.

COL. MARTIN. Was there a little boy sleeping in the next room?

LEO. I did you wrong! I did you a terrible, terrible wrong! Can I at least now say I'm sorry?

COL. MARTIN. 'Sorry' don't mean shit to *that little BOY*! That little boy who got left alive to *suffer*! Where's that gun?

FRITZ. Hold it, now, hold it –

LEO. No! Come on and kill me! Shoot me! I deserve it. I'm a worthless ugly piece of shit, so *DO IT*!

COL. MARTIN. Where's the gun? You! Give me that gun.

WINDSOR. No, no, I'm not giving you the gun…

COL. MARTIN. Give me the GUN! I'm going to kill the bastard!

WINDSOR. *I'll* shoot the son of a bitch!

COL. MARTIN. I have a *right* to shoot him! Now give me the *GODDAMN GUN*!

PAUL. *STOP!* Stop. Nobody can kill him.

PAUL *steps aside to reveal* LEO *lying very still.*

He's gone.

COL. MARTIN. Gone – ?

MARIANNE. Wait, what do you mean? Who's gone? You don't mean…?

PAUL. Leo is dead.

CLAUDIA. No…

FRITZ. I've never watched that happen before.

MARIANNE. He can't be – gone. He was only faking. And I called him a big baby. I have to apologize to him! *LEO!*

BISHOP. I'm sorry, Mrs Brink.

MARIANNE. He said he loved me. You heard him say it. Oh God, he looks so small…

PAUL. Bishop, do you want to say a few words, or – ?

BISHOP. I didn't really know the man very well…

A silence. No one knows what to say.

FRITZ. Leo Brink was never small. He was huge. And now what are we supposed to do? Who's going to tell us where to go for sunglasses in Stockholm? Or the best bok choy in Saigon? Leo had all the knowledge, he was… he was necessary. Something out there wanted Leo to be a part of all this. Part of us. We don't know why. So. Let's just miss him.

CLAUDIA. And then some.

ALL (*variously, not simultaneous*). Amen.

RAFFAEL. McGogg, the tapestry.

McGOGG *pulls down the TAPESTRY and covers* LEO.

MARIANNE. Thank you, Fritzie. Sorry. Fritz.

FRITZ. Fritzie's fine. Fritzie, Fritz, whatever.

THEY embrace. Then, MARIANNE *straightens the tapestry on* LEO, *tucking him in.*

CLAUDIA. We're next, you know. All of us. So who's gonna be first? Or, here's a thought: who's gonna *be LAST*? Will you just kill me now and get it over with? Please. Just do it. You know it's bound to happen.

PAUL. I know, baby. I know.

COL. MARTIN. The lady has a point.

FRITZ. How did we get here, anyway? Can somebody tell me where we went wrong?

RAFFAEL. Brunch! That was the fatal mistake. As always.

PAUL. No. The funeral at À La Mode. We shoulda turned back then.

FRITZ. Maybe if we didn't go to Zeno's…

SOLDIER. We met at Zeno's.

FRITZ. I'm factoring that in.

RAFFAEL. No, no, no. Coming here. *This*. This was the tragic error! That was when the gods frowned on us…! And you know what the ancients did. To release themselves, in such dilemmas.

PAUL. What…

RAFFAEL. They appeased the gods.

PAUL. Yeah, right! – They did?

RAFFAEL. Averting the catastrophe. Making things right again.

CLAUDIA. I'd do anything. I'll appease the gods.

RAFFAEL. There was only one way to do it. A scapegoat. A blood sacrifice.

BISHOP. Wait a moment, wait a moment.

RAFFAEL. When the sacred victim dies, the curse is lifted. The plague is cured.

FRITZ. *Stop!* This is delusion, people!

CLAUDIA. Be quiet, Fritz.

PAUL. So we just need a sacred victim.

RAFFAEL. Yes. Who will nobly give up his own life to save the others!

MARIANNE. And you'd do it, you'd do that for us, Raffi?

RAFFAEL. Actually, I was thinking – Windsor.

ALL EYES turn to WINDSOR.

WINDSOR. No, no. Don't look at me like that.

RAFFAEL. You have the weapon.

WINDSOR. No.

RAFFAEL. You want to be free, do you not? Of all this?

WINDSOR *scoffs quietly.*

Why do you laugh?

WINDSOR. You think 'the gods' would even hear the shot? If I was the victim? You gotta give up somebody significant. Somebody who's somebody.

WINDSOR *holds out the gun to* RAFFAEL.

Your Excellency.

A silence.

RAFFAEL. Windsor, Inferno, is right. (*Takes the gun.*) I will be the victim. I will be the goat! For once I will do something noble in my life.

FRITZ. Hang on, now, hang on, let's think about this.

RAFFAEL. No. The die is cast! (*Shakes off* FRITZ.) I thank you, my friends. For everything. Everyone, all of you. Now if you will just excuse me to the bathroom for a moment – *adidio*!

RAFFAEL *heads for the closet.*

MARIANNE. Raffi – wait. Don't move. Everybody stay exactly where you are.

FRITZ. What…

MARIANNE. No, no, stay there, Fritzie. It's sort of wonderful. How long have we been here? I don't know, I've lost touch. But how many times have we changed places in here? We've moved a thousand times – like pieces on a chessboard. But look! Right now – all of us – we're all exactly where we were that night! As we were leaving. Just before we decided to stay. We're at *Square One*. Or am I dreaming? Tell me. Somebody.

CLAUDIA. It's true. I was right here.

PAUL. I was here.

SOLDIER. Fritz was at my left.

MARIANNE. Leo was on the sofa – alive, but – on the sofa. Bishop, you were at the piano.

COL. MARTIN. What difference does any of this make?

MARIANNE. Who spoke first? Try to remember. Raffi, you said something.

RAFFAEL. I don't know…

MARIANNE. *Think.* Say it.

It slowly comes to RAFFAEL.

RAFFAEL. I said… 'Mimis amichichis, it has been a lovely day – *and* evening – but now I must wish you all a fond goodnight. And for now – adidio.'

They look around at each other trying to reconstruct that night. The pace of the following is deliberate, almost dreamlike.

MARIANNE. Paul, then you said –

PAUL. 'It was lovely, Raffi.'

A pause as CLAUDIA *tries to remember what she said.*

CLAUDIA. 'Perfect. And who cares about the meal, anyway?'

SHE air-kisses him on each cheek.

RAFFAEL. 'Your Holiness?'

BISHOP (*rising from the piano*). 'A truly joyful evening. God bless you, sir.'

MARIANNE. Leo said something, then I said does he have to say that all the time, then –

COL. MARTIN. 'Back to barracks, Lieutenant.'

SOLDIER. 'Fritz? One final look at the stars?'

FRITZ. 'If they're still there.'

A general CACOPHONY of goodbyes:

PAUL. Thanks, Raffi!
LEO. It was great!

CLAUDIA. Love you, sweetie!

MARIANNE. À tout à l'heure!

COL. MARTIN. An honor, sir!

BISHOP. Wonderful!

THEY collectively make for the portal. But –

THEY STOP just short of it. A moment of shock and dismay.

MARIANNE (*realizing they've stopped short again*). Oh, no…

PAUL. What's wrong?

FRITZ. What did we do wrong? What's missing?

A MOMENT.

LEO *BURPS resoundingly.*

THEY ALL turn around. LEO *sits up groggily.*

LEO. Who's hungry?

MARIANNE. Oh, darling, darling!

SHE embraces LEO.

LEO. Hiya, doll. Guess I must've blacked out, huh?

MARIANNE. Yes. Yes, it was probably those carrots.

LEO. Why am I covered in tapestry?

MARIANNE. Because, darling. *You deserve it.*

LEO. Oh. Okay… We going home soon?

MARIANNE. Any moment. Aren't we? Raffi?

RAFFAEL. Yes. Yes.

The BISHOP *happens to hit the piano keys and the piano starts to play.*

BISHOP. The piano…! It's playing!

COL. MARTIN. *Take your places!*

EVERYBODY gets into the proper place in the room.

And begin!

RAFFAEL. 'Mimis amichichis, it has been a lovely day – and evening – but I must wish you all a fond goodnight. And for now – adidio!'

WINDSOR *stands at the portal. They go through their lines more swiftly and urgently than before.*

PAUL. 'It was lovely, Raffi.'

CLAUDIA. 'Perfect. And who cares about the meal, anyway?'

RAFFAEL. 'Your Holiness?'

BISHOP. 'A truly joyful evening. God bless you, sir.'

MARIANNE. 'Time, Leo.' Leo, that's you.

LEO. 'Well – back to square one.'

MARIANNE. 'O, must he say that all the time?'

COL. MARTIN. 'Back to barracks, Lieutenant.'

SOLDIER. 'Fritz? One final look at the stars?'

FRITZ. 'If they're still there.'

MARIANNE. Let's go! Follow me, everyone!

ALL OF THEM, LEO *too, step through the portal. A moment of total silent amazement.*

THEIR CELLPHONES RING. THEY answer.

Simultaneous:

CLAUDIA. Hello? Yes, hello? Shiva, is that you?
PAUL (*to* CLAUDIA). Is it them, is it the kids?
RAFFAEL. Buenos didias! Or buenos nanoches!
SOLDIER. Hello, Mom? Mom, it's me!
LEO. Hello? Yes, we're fine! We're fine!
FRITZ. I don't know who you are, but hello!
COL. MARTIN. Josephine? Thank God!

CLAUDIA. It's Shiva! She says the kids are okay!

SHOUTS OF JOY as they hug each other, high-five, etc.

BISHOP. A miracle! A true miracle!

Then a moment of shocked silence as they realize they're actually out of The Room.

FRITZ. I don't hear any gunshots…

PAUL. I don't hear anything.

RAFFAEL. Nothing…!

CLAUDIA. Nothing's fine with me.

LEO. Did all that really happen?

MARIANNE. Something must have happened. Look at us.

THEY take in how ragged they are.

The COLONEL *blows his whistle.*

COL. MARTIN. Ladies and gentlemen, this is your Department of Homeland Security, signing off – until further notice!

RAFFAEL. Excuse me, Co-lo-nel. 'Further notice…'?

COL. MARTIN. *Until further notice.* Back to barracks, Lieutenant!

SOLDIER. Listen, Fritz.

FRITZ. No apologies. I was in there, too. And hey – you said you wanted real life.

COL. MARTIN. *On the double now, let's GO!*

As the SOLDIER *starts out:*

FRITZ. Take care of yourself, Soldier.

SOLDIER *and* COLONEL MARTIN *EXIT.*

It's funny. I never did learn his name…

BISHOP. I really have to thank you all. Of course, it was pretty darn harrowing in there. But I know what I am now.

MARIANNE. And what is that?

BISHOP. A priest. It just took a little practice. (*Spreads his arms in a very priestly blessing.*) Go in peace, my children.

BISHOP *STARTS OUT.*

MARIANNE. Your Grace – ?

MARIANNE *takes off her slippers and holds them out to him.*

A small donation.

BISHOP. God bless you, my child!

The BISHOP *EXITS, fondly holding* MARIANNE*'s slippers.*

RAFFAEL. And Windsor, I want to say…

THEY look around.

Where did he go?

PAUL. He's gone.

LEO. Not quite. He's still out there somewhere.

A pause as the group takes this in. MUSIC.

MARIANNE. Anyway – we're here. And it's a beautiful day.

CLAUDIA. Any day would be beautiful right now.

MARIANNE. Oh. My. God

CLAUDIA. You don't agree?

MARIANNE. No. I just realized. It hit me, looking at us. What that thing was, that important thing I was supposed to do!

CLAUDIA. Okay, so what was it?!

They wait a moment expectantly.

MARIANNE. Oh – nothing. I'll just do it.

ALL. Gaaaaaah!

LEO. I tell you, I'm the luckiest bastard in the whole wide world. Okay, so. Onwards, babe?

MARIANNE. Onwards.

MARIANNE takes his hand, to go.

CLAUDIA. Honey?

PAUL. You bet.

PAUL and CLAUDIA join hands.

MARIANNE. Raffi?

RAFFAEL. With pleasure.

RAFFAEL joins the others readying themselves to move on.

MARIANNE. Fritzie?

FRITZ. I don't think so. I've got a bunch of things to clean up. Like my life. Like my head. Like pretty much everything.

MARIANNE. Don't you be a stranger.

LEO. Okay. Well. Back to square one!

FRITZ starts out, changes her mind and turns back.

FRITZ. Oh, what the hell! La vidida ay la blahblah – whatever!

FRITZ joins them. The group is complete.

MARIANNE. All right, where do we want to eat?

They start to walk and the field beings to materialize behind them, perhaps more glorious than before.

But now we are aware of those GUNSHOTS again, EXPLOSIONS in the distance. THEY walk on, moving a little faster, looking over their shoulders. They walk faster… and faster… almost but not quite running now…

…going nowhere, as always, with brisk determination.

END.